Human Resources

Human Resources

Best Practices in Church Management

Carol L. Fowler

Paulist Press
New York / Mahwah, NJ

Cover image (background): lmichman/bigstock.com
Cover and book design by Dawn Massa, Lightly Salted Graphics

Library of Congress Cataloging-in-Publication Data is available upon request.

ISBN 978-0-8091-5313-8 (paperback)
ISBN 978-1-58768-652-8 (e-book)

Published by Paulist Press
997 Macarthur Boulevard
Mahwah, New Jersey 07430
www.paulistpress.com

Printed and bound in the
United States of America

Contents

This book is dedicated to the lay ecclesial ministers, clergy,
and vowed religious who prepared the way for all of us to value the
people who implement our mission, the mission of the gospel in our times
over the last fifty years. These pastoral leaders were the early change
agents and forged a new understanding and commitment to
justice in the church workplace.

About the Series

"The church is not a business!" Those of us who are involved in church management hear this comment on a regular basis. The appropriate response is, "Yes, it's true that the church is not a business, but we do have a stewardship responsibility to use our resources effectively. Frequently, that responsibility requires the utilization of sound business management techniques."

Canon law lists three priestly functions. Priests are responsible for teaching, sanctifying, and governing. Most priests relish their roles as teachers and sanctifiers, but few priests get excited over the parish governance tasks that are their responsibility. Very few men seek ordination because they want to run a small business.

While a parish isn't a business, governing a parish requires a significant number of management skills. Funds must be raised and bills must be paid, presumably under the guidance of a parish budget. Staff must be hired and provided with direction. The significant investment in parish facilities needs to be properly maintained. Church security, regarding both facilities and personnel, has become increasingly important. Parish planning is an on-going requirement. The pastor is expected to show leadership in a variety of areas. The list goes on. All these activities must be carried out within the constraints posed by both canon and civil laws.

In fact, the task of governing a parish has become even more challenging in recent years. Because of a number of factors, men are often assigned to administer larger and more complex parishes. Some are assigned as pastor of multiple parishes. In some cases, these multiple parishes are a great distance from one another. And in far too many cases, we are asking our priests to live alone.

Unfortunately, our seminaries are so overwhelmed with the educational requirements necessary to turn out priests that they are unable to make room in the curriculum to educate them as pastors. This may not have been a serious concern when the church was flush with priests and men would spend fifteen to twenty years serving as parochial vicars, in effect serving as apprentices and learning how to govern a parish. Today, however, it is not unusual for a priest to be assigned his first pastorate two or three years after ordination.

The good news is that, in many cases, pastors are assisted by a lay staff. But often the lay staff members themselves lack management training. They too struggle with budgets, managing volunteers, conflict resolution, planning for the future, and other management tasks.

Paulist Press has recognized the need for a series of educational materials to address the needs of church workers, both clergy and staff, who serve in a variety of management roles ranging from parishes to dioceses to social service organizations and who have no previous management experience. The result is this series on Best Practices in Church Management.

This series of books covers a wide range of functional church management areas, presented at a level of understanding intended for those church workers who find themselves with management responsibilities but little or no management education or experience. These are practical guides to parish management, not academic treatises. Jargon has been eliminated. Their purpose is to remove the anxiety from church management. These are the books that could be used in a seminary short course on parish management or presented to a newly appointed pastor. Parish, diocesan, and social service staff members with a background in areas such as theology, education, or social work who have suddenly been thrust into a management role will also find this series useful. Even those with some management background will appreciate the detailed discussions they will find in these books.

I am proud to be working with Paulist Press as the Best Practices in Church Management series editor. Paulist Press has a well-established reputation for turning out the finest in educational materials to serve the church. This series is no exception. We have been able to attract national experts in each of a variety of functional management fields to share their wisdom. We hope you will find each book to be an invaluable guide as you carry out your stewardship in service to the church.

Charles Zech, PhD
Professor Emeritus of Church Management
Villanova University

Foreword

Imagine a farmer going out to sow some seed. As he sowed, some seeds fell on the edge of the path and were trampled on, and the birds of the air ate them up. Some others fell on patches of rock where they found little soil, and when they came up, they withered up because they had no moisture. Some other seeds fell among thorns, and the thorns grew with them and choked them. And some seeds fell into rich ground, and they grew and produced an enormous crop.

Listen, anyone who has ears to hear!

—See Matthew 13:4–9

Anyone in pastoral leadership these days knows how important it is to be rooted and centered. Solid grounding in faith and spirituality accompanied by the knowledge and exercise of solid administrative and human resource practices comprise the rich soil that nurtures the unfolding mission. Nowhere is this more important than in a parish setting. Unfortunately, given the constraints of time and the demands of theological preparation, substantive education in management practices is often insufficient. This can result in a pastor functioning on a shaky administrative foundation. Consequently, many have found themselves caught in personnel and financial situations that might otherwise have been avoided. Such situations result in time spent in repairing human resource problems or legal issues—time that could otherwise be spent directed toward the realization of the pastoral mission.

In evaluating exemplary leaders in the faith community, what is overwhelmingly apparent is these leaders possess the capacity to meld a solid foundation in the gospel with a strong capacity to relate with others and meticulous attention to ethical business practices. In the body of literature of adult relational theory, the best leaders in any profession are those who have a strong sense of inner authority matched by a strong positive relationship with other people. Such secure leaders soar when they also exhibit administrative competence.

Carol Fowler presents a clear, practical, and compelling path forward for those seeking to be excellent pastoral leaders. She accomplishes this with amazing practicality coupled with a firm grounding in Catholic social teaching. While the book focuses on parish administration, it is easily applicable to the formation of leaders across the spectrum of faith-based ministries in our churches. Hiring processes, benefits, compensation, and a variety of issues a pastoral leader faces are presented within the framework of best practices in human resource management.

The ongoing development of successful, secure pastors who are equipped with solid information in human resource practices till the soil for the rich planting and thriving of the gospel.

Donna Markham, OP, PhD
President and CEO
Catholic Charities USA

Acknowledgments

What does the LORD require of you
but to do justice, and to love kindness,
and to walk humbly with your God?
—Micah 6:8

I once had the privilege of working with a gifted leader, Bishop John Gorman, who believed and practiced his theory that whatever we are doing alone, we could do better with others. As I undertook the challenge of writing a book, this worldview echoed in my life, almost daily.

I have been gifted with family, friends, colleagues, and mentors who supported and encouraged my development as a person, lay ecclesial minister, administrator, and now erstwhile author.

I learned and witnessed justice in ministry while a vowed and now associate member of the Adrian Dominican Sisters. I experienced justice and pastoral excellence in ministry from my friend, pastor, and mentor, Rev. Thomas McDevitt of the Diocese of Lansing, Michigan. The Pastoral Team at St. John Student Parish in East Lansing, Michigan, struggled and shaped much of my current understanding of justice in the church workplace with a special acknowledgment of my colleague and friend Elizabeth Schweitzer, who was the administrator/business manager in that parish for many years.

In the Archdiocese of Chicago, I was privileged to work with two gifted archbishops, Joseph Cardinal Bernardin and Francis Cardinal George, OMI. My twenty-five years in the archdiocese provided countless moments of grace, growth, and challenge. I am especially grateful to my colleague Fred Van Den Hende, who taught me and collaborated with all at the archdiocese to provide excellence in human resources. I was honored to work with gifted and dedicated people in the Department of Personnel Services for more than twenty-one years.

There are two people to whom I will always be enormously grateful: Daniel Gast and Dr. Peter Gilmour walked me through every step of the process. They edited, made suggestions, and, most of all, provided unending encouragement. I am also grateful to Charles Zech, Professor Emeritus of Villanova University, who conceived of and created this series on church management, and Donna Crilly, editor at Paulist Press, who has implemented his vision.

> I thank my God every time I remember you, constantly praying with joy in every one of my prayer for all of you, because of your sharing in the gospel from the first day until now. (Phil 1:3–5)

Introduction

Working with people toward a common goal with a shared vision is rewarding beyond measure yet challenging beyond words. For these reasons, I want to share my experience and insights in this book about church human resources. My objective is not to create a whole new group of human resources professionals. Pastors and church leaders do not need to become experts in human resources. Neither should they become anxious when they lack human resources expertise. Likewise, it is not my purpose to impose business practices that feel onerous or out of context in faith-based organizations. The thoughtless imposition of business practices creates complications and feels inappropriate in a church setting.

However, implementing sound business practices in faith-based organizations *in ways that respect and value our religious identity* is critical. We need to look at the best practices in management that move us to effective implementation of our strategic plans. The purpose of this book is to inform pastors and designated leaders about a significant body of human resources knowledge. We must use this information to achieve excellence in management that faithfully serves mission. All leaders need to know how to access this information, what resources are available to them as leaders, and when they should seek assistance from a human resources professional or a labor attorney.

This book is about the infrastructure of human resources, spanning the legal, informational, and procedural dimensions of the field. It is limited, however, as a basic manual for faith-based organizations. It does not provide comprehensive human resources information because for the book's intended audience that is not necessary. Its chapters provide basic information, terminology, and direction for new or experienced pastors or church leaders. They contain recommended tools and best practices for dealing with the human resources issues that face every parish and faith-based organization. The intended audience includes parish pastors, business managers, school principals, pastoral ministers responsible for coordinating and supervising staff and volunteers, directors of church-related offices and agencies, and others who manage faith-based organizations without the "luxury" of a human resources department or director.

Learning to manage and lead people is a life-long endeavor. One book or one leadership experience fails to achieve all-inclusive information and proficiency. We learn about leading people from our coaches and mentors, by experiences of being managed and managing, by formal learning experiences, and by our successes and failures. However, becoming familiar with basic information and tools yields a foundation for dealing with some of the everyday challenges of managing and ministering with people.

I have had the privilege of providing basic human resources training to many parish and church leaders across the country, and even in more distant locations, including Kenya, Germany, and Italy. I have worked with pastors, school principals, parish business managers, priests who will soon be appointed as pastors, organization directors, seminarians, deacons, campus ministers, pastoral administrators, and other lay and ordained leaders. They each and all desire to work with people effectively and help everyone succeed. They are particularly faith and mission driven people, whom I hope will find this book helpful as they review basic structures and best practices in church human resources.

This book is the third book of a series on church management from Villanova University School of Business at the Center for Church Management. The first in the series is *Parish Finance: Best Practices in Church Management* by Michael J. Castrilli and Charles E. Zech. The second book is *Pastoral Leadership: Best Practices for Church Leaders*. With the series in mind, this book has similar goals and organization as well as a parish case study.

Goals and Objectives

The overarching goal of this book is to help you work with people effectively and pastorally to achieve the mission of the church through the ministry of your parish, school, or organization. The objectives are the following:

- To be **practical**: To provide outcome-oriented methods and results for church leaders.
- To be **accessible**: To clarify key terminology and legislation and provide tools and ideas for implementation of excellent human resources practices.
- To be **resourceful**: To provide resources, tools, and information that are useful in pastoral settings.
- To be **pastoral**: To consistently reference all protocols, recommendations, resources, policies, approaches, and systems to the faith-based context in which we serve.

Organization

1. Foundations of Church Human Resources

The basic infrastructure of human resources for faith-based organizations is focused on the pastoral and theological foundations of working with staff and volunteers followed by the civil, legal, and policy structures on which best practices rely.

2. The Employment Relationship

The staff and volunteer relationship begins with the recruiting and hiring process. It continues with establishing the culture and milieu in which people serve, as well as the leadership styles and values consistent with the parish or organization. Communication processes, conflict management, and conduct of meetings are factors in establishing the work-related relationships throughout the organization. Decisions and rationale applied to performance management, compensation, and benefits are all part of establishing positive ongoing employment relationships that nurture ministerial excellence.

3. Managing Transitions and Terminations

Change is difficult in much of life, and faith-based employment settings are no exception. How we prepare for and manage transitions must align with our mission and our pastoral identity, supported by legal expertise and the skills we cultivate in applying human resources practices as church leaders.

4. Pastors' Frequently Asked Questions

This section features some of the questions most often voiced by new pastors and those taking pastoral assignments in unfamiliar parish settings.

St. Michael's Parish Case Study

To introduce each topic, this guide will view the topics to be discussed through the eyes of Fr. Dave, a newly appointed pastor to St. Michael's Parish. This is the same Fr. Dave who was introduced to us in the Castrilli and Zech, *Parish Finance: Best Practices in Church Management*. To provide a better base for a discussion of church human resources, I make some additions and modifications to the parish description.

Introduction to Fr. Dave

Fr. Dave is at a crossroads. He has been blessed by a new opportunity, but with it come new and unfamiliar challenges. He is a diocesan priest, just beginning his first assignment as a pastor. He loves the spiritual ministry of his work, but now he is finding much more is expected of him.

Fr. Dave is four years out of seminary. During his formation, he learned much about what it takes to be a successful priest, but he learned virtually nothing about what it takes to be a successful pastor. His seminary did not offer a single course on parish administration, leaving him in the dark on many basic financial and operational issues. Moreover, such issues never came up during his formation or in spiritual direction. It seems everyone assumed he would be introduced to pastoring during the early years of his priesthood by apprenticeship to a senior priest.

Unfortunately, when Fr. Dave was a parochial vicar, the senior priest controlled nearly every element of parish operations. Fr. Dave was not included in many duties, like talks with the parish business manager or meetings with the parish finance council. Even after several years in the parish, Fr. Dave did not know much more about the administrative side of pastoring than he had when he started.

But God had plans for Fr. Dave. When one of the diocese's pastors died unexpectedly, the bishop had no choice but to appoint Fr. Dave as a pastor of a midsize parish, despite his obvious lack of preparation. The stakes are high: his new parish needs significant financial cleanup, and a contractor has completed construction plans to renovate the parish hall, some of which are already in the works.

This new role will involve much more than the prayers, homilies, and parishioner visits he so enjoys. Fr. Dave is now administrator and a manager, faced with the legal and fiduciary responsibilities that come with financial oversight. It is certainly not how he planned it, but Fr. Dave quickly realizes that he will have to learn to be pastor through on-the-job training.[1]

St. Michael's Parish Profile

St. Michael's is a large parish of 2,500 families in a suburban setting. The parish has a small elementary school, with a principal, teachers, and school secretary, as well as parish administrative and ministerial staff, including a pastoral associate, director of faith formation, director of liturgy and music, business manager, maintenance person, a part-time janitor to clean the school each day, and a parish receptionist/secretary.

1 See Michael J. Castrilli and Charles E. Zech, *Parish Finance: Best Practices in Church Management* (Mahwah, NJ: Paulist Press, 2016), xv.

1

Pastoral Foundations of Church Human Resources

Chapter Preview

In this chapter, Fr. Dave will:

- Compare best human resources practices in business organizations and best practices in faith-based organizations.
- Examine Scripture and Catholic social teaching as the pastoral foundations of the church workplace.
- Recognize the relationship of faith-based community mission with best practices in human resources.

Best Human Resources Practices in Business and Church

As church leaders mature in their management and administration practices, they willingly and even enthusiastically adopt best practices from the business world. By adopting proven methodologies, they critically advance their organizations' and communities' effectiveness. Effective church leaders know that good management requires solid financial skills and legal accounting practices. Churches and religious nonprofits also engage in solid planning processes to promote their future effectiveness as organizations. Their fund development practices, also known as stewardship, draw from best practices of the nonprofit world. Churches work very hard, for instance, to attain sustainability by developing donation portfolios. As church organizations seek the money that grows their missions, they grow in stature by adopting accountability and transparency practices that attract financial support. The business disciplines of marketing and communication become critical to churches as they compete for attention amid the distractions and hyperactivity of modern life.

EFFECTIVE CHURCH LEADERS KNOW THAT GOOD MANAGEMENT REQUIRES SOLID FINANCIAL SKILLS AND LEGAL ACCOUNTING PRACTICES.

Church Identity and Human Resources

Human resources (HR) might be the last area in which churches implement best practices. In the past, churches, church organizations, and even dioceses sometimes operated under the false notion that constitutional separation of church and state meant labor laws don't apply. Eventually, it becomes clear that labor laws *do* apply to churches and church organizations. We as church leaders are accountable to the legal system for implementation of lawful and just HR policies.

CHURCH LEADERS ARE ACCOUNTABLE TO THE LEGAL SYSTEM FOR IMPLEMENTATION OF LAWFUL AND JUST HR POLICIES.

There are several reasons human resources practices are often adopted more slowly by church organizations. Many church organizations are small, and have exceptionally specialized missions. Volunteers and small staffs perform much of the work. It is tempting to dismiss best practices in human resources from the business world because these practices don't seem to apply when we are talking about clergy, men and women religious, and laity in ministerial positions.

Many of us resist adopting human resources policies and practices because we do not see them as compatible with who we are as church. We may even see the mission of the church and best HR practices as antithetical. However, best business practices in human resources actually bolster and align with the mission of any particular industry or organization. A vice-president for human resources therefore becomes a significant position in every business—and, today, in many dioceses. That senior-level executive takes responsibility for establishing and aligning all the work of human resources with the mission, goals, and values of the organization. Effective HR policies and practices support and enable the people who make up the employment base of the organization. That is precisely what we are called to do as church. We do well when we skillfully utilize human resources to achieve full realization of mission as well as the human potential of ministers, employees, and volunteers. It is the premise of this book that the best practices in human resources developed in the business and nonprofit sectors of our society deserve skillful adaptation within the religious sectors of our society as well.

To achieve that, we must begin by being clear about the pastoral foundations of the church organization where we work, whether that organization is a Catholic parish or diocese; a small church-related organization or a large one like Catholic Charities; a church-affiliated hospital, school, or social service agency. As church organizations, we are called to serve the people of God effectively and comprehensively by promoting the gospel of Jesus Christ, by serving the poor, and by advocating for justice in all aspects of society. Pope Francis calls on us to be a church of mercy. His mandate is for us to preach and be people of the Word, people impelled by the joy of the gospel to lives of evangelization and service.

WE ARE CALLED TO SERVE THE PEOPLE OF GOD EFFECTIVELY AND COMPREHENSIVELY BY PROMOTING THE GOSPEL OF JESUS CHRIST, BY SERVING THE POOR, AND BY ADVOCATING FOR JUSTICE IN ALL ASPECTS OF SOCIETY.

Scripture and Catholic Social Teaching

As we survey the pastoral foundations of church employment, we might begin by seeking out instances in Scripture that deal with work or labor and management. There are many, but perhaps the well-known parable of the workers in the vineyard would come to mind. Another with intriguing similarities is that of the prodigal son. Both stories tell us that our God cares little about legalities of hiring, placement, or compensation. Rather, the stories emphasize God's almost scandalous generosity while suggesting that God values the "last and least" as much as the "first and steadfast." That is a high standard we ought to take to heart, but only as we consider possible unintended consequences in today's workplaces when we confuse misplaced generosity and principles of equity.

Some employment practices intended to show generosity to some employees might inadvertently take advantage of others. For example, a church organization may have a staff member who performs poorly, comes late, and leaves early, but she is the sole provider for her family or has a sick spouse. The pastor or manager therefore accommodates the shortcomings of this staff member and may in fact even reward her with compensation increases. However, these accommodations may have a negative effect on the other staff members, have an impact on morale, and may even constitute illegal discrimination. Pastoral sensitivity and outreach to staff members having trouble that affects their ability to do their job is always appropriate but should not be confused with good employment practices. There is a creative tension between best practices in human resources and the identity of our faith-based organizations. By being attentive to this tension, we can practice excellent human resources principles yet do so while maintaining our fundamental church identity. The pastoral foundations of church HR are constructed out of scriptural references from both the Old and New Testaments, and in the modern era from Catholic social teaching well over a century in the making, as we will briefly review.[1]

Pope Leo XIII, in his landmark 1891 encyclical *Rerum Novarum*, On the Rights and Duties of Capital and Labor, outlined key principles of labor that needed focus and affirmation because of the Industrial Revolution.[2] Pope Leo understood the plight of workers at that time and knew that the church had to address the dire conditions in which many people around the world worked and lived. He strongly stated the principle that work must reflect the value and dignity of the human person. Pope Leo identified key factors for promoting the dignity of a human person as a worker. These included fair wages, safe working conditions, protections for working children, and time off on Sundays for the expression of religious obligations. The second key principle of *Rerum Novarum* complemented the obligation of recognizing the dignity of the human person by challenging workers themselves to focus on the common good, larger society, and conscientious contributions to the workplace. On the ninetieth anniversary of *Rerum Novarum* in 1981, Pope John Paul II reaffirmed the principal in *Laborem Exercens* (On Human Work).[3] He addressed the encyclical well beyond the traditional audience of hierarchs and patriarchs, writing to "all Sons and Daughters of the Church, and all Men and Women of good will."

WORK MUST REFLECT THE VALUE AND DIGNITY OF THE HUMAN PERSON.

1. For scriptural references to Catholic social teaching, access the U.S Bishops' *Catholic Social Teaching Scripture Guide* at the USCCB website at http://www.usccb.org/beliefs-and-teachings/how-we-teach/catholic-education/campus-ministry/tools-for-action/upload/cst-scripture-guide-donna-update-matt2.pdf (accessed February 6, 2019).

2. The Vatican website has official English translations of many papal documents. *Rerum Novarum*, the Encyclical of Pope Leo XIII on Capital and Labor, issued May 15, 1891, is accessible at http://w2.vatican.va/content/leo-xiii/en/encyclicals/documents/hf_l-xiii_enc_15051891_rerum-novarum.html. *Rerum Novarum* means "Of New Things."

3. See http://w2.vatican.va/content/john-paul-ii/en/encyclicals/documents/hf_jp-ii_enc_14091981_laborem-exercens.html.

With that sense of inclusiveness, Catholic social teaching promotes active participation by everyone in the running of an organization to the extent appropriate for the organization's mission and the workers' abilities. One clear application of this principle is the right of workers to participate in worker organizations, associations, and unions. The Catholic Church has explicitly supported the rights of workers to organize in our society. Consequently, church officials often struggle to promote the right to organize within the realm of church employment. There are examples of successful union organization in American church organizations such as hospitals, a few schools, Catholic universities, and Catholic cemeteries, and among maintenance and service workers in dioceses and parishes.

Nevertheless, the principle of active participation is broader than unionization. Workers' participation in decisions that affect their work is encouraged and even required, to the extent possible, in an ethical church employment situation. Many businesses recognize the advantage of having full participation and cooperative effort at every level of their organizations, observes William J Byron, SJ, in his book *The Power of Principles*.[4] For example, Boeing Company makes clear in its values handbook that the company will foster participation, cooperation, and as much shared decision-making as a given situation allows. As church organizations, our own social teaching tells us that a participative workplace greatly enhances the effectiveness of our church and organizational mission. If we truly believe in the dignity of the human person, we will also believe in the dignity of human work and the role each person plays as a significant contributor to work and mission.

Catholic social teaching is an especially rich resource informing human resources in any church workplace. In 1998, the Catholic Bishops of the United States issued a brilliant summary of the church's social teaching, encapsulated in seven themes. The themes interrelate, and so are worth listing here. As you review, note how the issues of work, family, and creation interconnect.

Seven Principles of Catholic Social Teaching

1. Dignity of the Human Person
2. Call to Family, Community, and Participation
3. Rights and Responsibilities
4. Preferential Option for and with People Who Are Poor
5. Dignity of Work and the Rights of Workers
6. Solidarity
7. Care for God's Creation

Reference materials for study and discussion can be found at the U.S. Conference of Catholic Bishops website, www.usccb.org, and by contacting the Catholic Charities Office for Social Justice in St. Paul, Minnesota, at osj@cctwincities.org.

The church has consistently upheld the rights and needs of both workers and organizations. For over forty years, the National Association of Church Personnel Administrators (NACPA) has actively supported best HR practices in the Catholic Church in the United States. This organization's mission is to work toward justice in the church workplace, in keeping with the social teaching of the church. One of

4. William Byron, *The Power of Principles: Ethics for the New Corporate Culture* (New York: Orbis Books, 2006).

the great insights of Catholic social teaching and of the NACPA is that justice is always relational and reciprocal. The association's goal is to seek justice for workers *and* for church organizations, and all are welcome to seek out NACPA resources and services.

Chapter Summary: Organizational Mission and Best Practices in Human Resources

In all organizations, the effectiveness of people's work depends on how well they know, understand, and implement the mission of the organization. Connection and commitment to church mission is vital for the successful management of people. As church, we have the great gift of a divinely inspired mission. Our mission comes from the gospel. We have been given the mandate to go, make disciples of all nations, and baptize in the name of Jesus (Matt 28:18–20). *We* are called to make disciples! Those disciples, in turn, become apostles. The foundation of the word *apostle* means to be sent into the world to continue two thousand years of evangelization. Those who work in a church, either as staff or as volunteers, are all called to this profound mission. They deserve the encouragement and support of their leaders, ordained and lay.

A church leader must pay attention to his own formation and development in mission if he is to form disciples, beginning with paid staff or volunteers in key positions. No one should take it for granted that once initial formation is completed, she has made an unwavering commitment to mission that can't possibly wane. Prayer, study, and participation in communities of belief enable the continued deepening and development of a leader's sense of mission. Then it becomes palpable and attractive to others.

Therefore, management of people is an expression of church mission. The way we treat, manage, and lead must manifest our very identity as church. Employees and volunteers in our church organizations, whether in diocesan offices, parishes, charitable organizations, or service agencies, are watching. They witness how leadership works with, values, and treats people. If we want people to believe that the mission is what we are about, then everything we do must exemplify how mission matters in our own daily lives. We can't say our organization values the poor, the marginalized, and the struggling, and in a moment of crisis conduct a massive layoff of employees with scant implementation of respect for human dignity, fairness, or understanding. Yes, there are times we may need to reduce staff. It can become a mission-critical function in any church organization, but how we reduce staff will be watched very carefully. If we are to be credible as implementers of mission, then we must manifest that in everything we do. That includes how we treat our staff, in times of plenty or scarcity.

It is our premise that we who are church leaders can exercise human resources practices effectively and efficiently while still retaining our identity as church. We recognize that when we strive for justice in the church workplace, justice is always a two-way street. Workplace justice values the individual employee and the volunteer. At the same time, justice toward the organization, supporting the common good, and guiding the mission must all factor into the equation. Hard decisions that weigh the rights and welfare of an individual with the welfare and integrity of the mission can at times be heart wrenching. But plain and simple, there will be occasions when any leader in a church setting must embrace that responsibility. In the chapters ahead, we hope to demonstrate how we can build just, mission-focused practices within our church settings. We begin by looking at key legal foundations that support best church human resources practices.

In chapter 2, we look at key legal foundations that support best practices in human resources in church settings.

2

Civil and Legal Foundations

Chapter Preview

In this chapter, Fr. Dave will:

- Learn basic legal rationale regarding employment practices.
- Examine equal employment opportunity, provisions of the Fair Labor Standards Act, and definitions of *employees* and *employers*.
- Survey other legal issues and legislation that apply to the church workplace.

Introduction

Church human resources practices function in our American society in the same ways as in secular and business organizations. *Separation of church and state does not exempt church organizations from the just and legal requirements of our society.* A culture of litigation pervades the United States, and the most litigious group is employees. Church organizations are not exempt from this reality.

As we begin this chapter on civil and legal foundations, it is important to note that this is general legal information. It is not meant to substitute for any specific advice, consultation, or interpretation you receive from your attorneys on legal matters pertaining to specific human resources cases.

SEPARATION OF CHURCH AND STATE DOES NOT EXEMPT CHURCH ORGANIZATIONS FROM THE JUST AND LEGAL REQUIREMENTS OF OUR SOCIETY.

Dioceses, parishes, schools, and other church organizations have different legal and corporate structures and charters. These specific structures strongly influence the interpretation of legal policies and processes. For example, about half of the Roman Catholic dioceses in this country are legally designated as Corporation Sole. Other dioceses are organized with parishes as individual corporations and set up with a variety of legal requirements for boards of directors or trustees. How a school, organization, church, or diocese is organized affects the specific interpretations of how laws are applied. For example, in California, employment laws are often significantly more restrictive and unique than in the rest of the states. With such exceptions noted, we will discuss those laws and legal best practices with general influence and importance for all church organizations.

A few of the most significant laws that affect our legal requirements as church employers include the following:

- Title VII of the Civil Rights Act of 1964
- ADEA (Age Discrimination in Employment Act)
- ADA (Americans with Disabilities Act)
- FLSA (Fair Labor Standards Act)
- IRCA (Immigration Reform and Control Act)
- FMLA (Family and Medical Leave Act)

Equal Employment Opportunity

Title VII of the Civil Rights Act of 1964 promotes equal employment opportunity. Title VII prohibits employers from discriminating based on race, color, religion, gender, or national origin in any employment practices, including hiring, termination, discipline, compensation, training, promotion, benefits, as well as the terms and conditions and privileges of employment. Only a few parishes are exempt from the Civil Rights Act. These are parishes that are individually incorporated and have fewer than fifteen employees. However, the provisions of Title VII are generally applicable to most church organizations. Even when we are legally exempt, social justice calls us to respect and uphold these antidiscrimination measures in every way possible.

The only exception to the Civil Rights Act for church organizations is that we may discriminate based on religion. Most church employers would only discriminate in hiring for those positions in which being a member of that faith is a key part of the function of the position. For example, the director of catechesis or youth ministry should be a member of the denomination that sponsors the church organization.

We may not discriminate against any ethnic group, race, or nationality in hiring, promotions, or terminations. For example, we can require language skills, but we may not discriminate because that person speaks the language with a nonnative accent. We may not discriminate based on nationality or race. The requirement is that we hire the most qualified person for the position regardless of race, nationality, or ethnic group.

Affirmative Action is not the same as Equal Employment Opportunity, although sometimes you might hear the terms incorrectly used interchangeably. The purpose of Affirmative Action is to make the workplace reflect the diversity of the community using deliberate actions. Equal Employment Opportunity requires that the employer not discriminate against minorities in hiring and employment practices. Some federal contractors are required to file Affirmative Action plans, but these requirements rarely affect church workplaces.

Equal Employment Opportunity legislation also prohibits discrimination based on sex. Women have been historically discriminated against in compensation, hiring, and promotions, and have often been treated disrespectfully or even sexually harassed. In interviewing for hiring or promotions, a common pattern of discrimination excludes women from opportunities because employers think women may take maternity leaves, stay home to take care of sick children, and so on. Some may believe that women consider work to be secondary in their priorities. Employers betray such prejudice when they ask questions such as, "Who will take care of your children if you are offered this position?" or "What does your husband think about you applying for this job?" From a pro-family church perspective and a justice perspective, this is neither a moral or faithful stance for a church employer. In U.S. law, women are a protected class of employees and must be treated equally in every aspect of employment. There is no place for sex discrimination in a hiring decision. Furthermore, this means not only paying women the same as men who perform the same work, but also making all positions in the organization available to women on an equal basis, if ordination is not a requirement for the position. The right of church organizations to discriminate based on religion also provides the church the right to decide who may or may not be ordained.

The *Age Discrimination in Employment Act* (ADEA) prohibits discrimination based on a person's age. Anyone over the age of forty is included in the provisions of this legislation. Mandatory retirement age is prohibited except for those that have a bona fide occupational qualification such as airline pilots, firefighters, or some top executives. This prohibition is violated even if the employer initiates the conversation regarding an employee's retirement. Sometimes, in an attempt to be pastoral, a church leader might suggest retirement to an employee, thereby avoiding having to terminate the employee for poor performance. However, such an approach is considered discriminatory based on age and violates the Age Discrimination in Employment Act. ADEA also prohibits employers from reducing benefits for older workers by forcing that person to participate in Medicare rather than the employer health plan or by not continuing to fund the pension plan of someone over the age of sixty-five or at any other age, if the employee continues to work and continues to meet the eligibility requirements established for younger workers. Attention to the provisions of this legislation are necessary in hiring, promotion, reorganization, and involuntary terminations.

The Americans with Disabilities Act (ADA) prohibits discrimination against people with physical or mental disabilities unless that disability prevents the potential employee from performing one of the essential functions of the job as named in the job description. If a reasonable accommodation can be made that allows that person to perform the job with assistance, the person should be hired without regard to the disability. Examples of these accommodations include devices such as a magnified screen for the computer or a wheelchair ramp into the building.

Fair Labor Standards Act

As we look at legal principles affecting church organizations, it is important to understand certain definitions that describe employers and employees. The first definition is contained in the *Fair Labor Standards Act* (FLSA). FLSA defines two kinds of employees, *exempt* and *nonexempt*, that is, employees who are exempt from FLSA and those who are not. FLSA is the federal legislation that requires some employees to be paid overtime for work beyond forty hours in a workweek. Staff persons employed in a bona fide executive, administrative, or professional capacity are exempt from the requirements for overtime pay. The executive exemption applies to those who supervise two or more people and have the authority to hire, fire, discipline, or make salary decisions for staff. This professional employee exemption is for those who perform work requiring advanced knowledge that is predominantly professional in character. In churches and schools, the positions that are normally exempt include teachers, principals, business managers, lay ecclesial ministers, and others having supervisory authority. All other positions are nonexempt. These include maintenance staff, secretaries, bookkeepers, teacher aides, and library aides. For these positions, each place of employment must keep accurate records of all work performed and the number of hours each nonexempt staff member works. Each hour worked must be paid, and time-and-a-half must be paid for each hour worked over forty in the workweek. We will discuss some of the details of recordkeeping and hourly compensation in the chapter on payroll practices.

In the federal wage and hour division handbook, clergy and members of religious orders who are serving in a church organization for religious purposes are not to be considered employees and are therefore not subject to FLSA. This is a ministerial exemption and is currently under review for others in ministry such as lay ecclesial ministers. In addition to the exemption for those in ministry, teachers and vowed religious are exempt from the salary threshold provisions.

There is a salary threshold that was to be raised as of December 1, 2016, to $913 per week or $47,476 per year. This figure will be adjusted every three years beginning on January 1, 2020. This means that in addition to the "duties tests" as defined in FLSA, to be considered exempt, the salary threshold requirement must be met. For example, a business manager who meets the administrative or professional duties requirement but does not earn $47,476 per year remains nonexempt and must meet the recordkeeping requirements for hourly employees. Nonexempt staff must be paid for every hour worked and be paid overtime when they work more than forty hours in a week. This legislation is under review as of the writing of this text.

Other critical definitions for understanding legal foundations are those that describe types of *employers*. Most state constitutions define employers as *at-will employers*. At-will employers reserve the right under state law to terminate any employee for any reason, with or without notice, and with or without cause, where such termination is not discriminatory. Discriminatory actions will be delineated a little later in this chapter. *Just-cause employers* take corrective action, including termination, only for clear, compelling, and justifiable reasons. These distinctions between types of employers have legal ramifications that are best left to attorneys. However, our premise in this book is that we believe we can do human resources in church in a way that reflects who we are as church. We should always strive to be just-cause employers. At-will employment may be a tool that is useful to attorneys in the defense of a case, but those of us who are employers and supervisors in the church workplace, need to think of ourselves as just-cause employers. Our self-understanding as just-cause employers is part and parcel of our employment decisions such as whom we hire, whom we promote, how we do performance management, and how we organize and reorganize our places of employment.

Miscellaneous Legislation and Legal Concerns

The *Immigration Reform and Control Act* (IRCA) is a federal law that is sometimes difficult for churches to implement. The plight of undocumented workers is a major concern of the church for humanitarian and pastoral reasons. The church is prominent among groups actively and vigorously advocating for immigration reform. However, we are still subject to the existing laws that make it illegal for anyone to knowingly employ someone who is not legally authorized to work in the United States. Penalties for violation of IRCA include heavy fines and may even result in imprisonment. Sometimes pastors and other church employers have tried to avoid IRCA by paying cash to undocumented workers. However, this is not the answer to our pastoral dilemma. In fact, paying in cash simply adds more violations to the list. If the employer or the employee does not pay proper taxes for employment arrangements, even more complications arise. At this point, we can most help undocumented workers by working to get them legal assistance, and by referring them to Catholic Charities and other organizations for assistance until they can become documented to work legally in the United States.

The *Family and Medical Leave Act* (FMLA) provides up to twelve weeks in any twelve-month period for the birth, adoption, or foster care placement of a child, for care of a spouse, child, or parent with a serious health condition, or for the employee's own serious health condition. This leave may be taken either in one block or intermittently. While on FMLA leave, the employee is unpaid and the employer continues to provide benefits on the same basis as before the employee began the leave. Employees on FMLA must be allowed to return to the same job or job of equal pay and status at the end of their leave, but generally may be terminated if they do not return after twelve weeks of leave. This can be complicated to implement and manage, so the guidance of someone with human resources expertise is very helpful. If you are in a diocese or organization with a human resources department, the director of that department will be able to assist the school principal or the pastor or the director of the church organization in implementing the family medical leave provisions.

Nepotism refers to the practice of allowing relatives to work for the same employer. Nepotism may limit diversity in an organization because, often, minorities are not appropriately represented at all levels within an organization, and the hiring of relatives of current employees tends to perpetuate the disparity. For a variety of reasons, many employers do not prohibit the hiring of relatives. However, most employers prohibit the employment of family members in supervisory/subordinate relationships, or in positions where working with relatives could allow one to cover up the misdeeds of the other or might invite the appearance of impropriety.

When employees report to family members, there can be conflicts when it becomes necessary to address poor performance or misconduct.

Sexual harassment results from a lack of respect for gender diversity in the workplace, and faith-based workplaces are not immune from this problem. The Equal Employment Opportunity Commission (EEOC) defines sexual harassment as the following:

> Unwelcome sexual advances, requests for sexual favors, and other verbal or physical conduct of a sexual nature, constitute sexual harassment when submission to or rejection of this conduct explicitly or implicitly affects an individual's employment, unreasonably interferes with an individual's work performance, or creates an intimidating, hostile, or offensive work environment.[1]

The two basic types of sexual harassment are quid pro quo and hostile work environment. *Quid pro quo* is most often perpetrated by a supervisor of some other authority figure who has the power to positively or negatively affect one's pay, benefits, eligibility for promotion, career path, or other aspect of one's employment. It generally involves promising some favorable treatment if the employee submits to the harassment or threatening some negative consequence if the employee rejects the harassment.

Hostile work environment sexual harassment usually does not involve the promise of rewards or the threat of consequences. It can be perpetrated by supervisors, coworkers, vendors, clients, parishioners, and so on. This type of harassment might include repeated requests for sexual favors, use of offensive language, sexually oriented conversations or jokes, unwanted or "accidental" touching, or the display of sexually oriented pictures, signs, or novelties.

As the designated leader of your organization you must be proactive in stopping any kind of sexual harassment. When you witness offensive items, pictures, behaviors, or language, you need to act. You should not wait until there is a complaint. It is also critical that all members of your staff know how to report sexual harassment and what expectations they can have of results, resolution, and confidentiality.

There are other types of harassment that also create hostile work environments. These include threatening or belittling actions toward staff and volunteers that are harmful, may cause worker failures, and contribute to stress-related physical and emotional symptoms.[2]

The Health Insurance Portability and Accountability Act (HIPPA) has resulted in many changes in protocols at pharmacies and doctor's offices. This act is designed to offer high levels of protection to every individual's right to privacy regarding health information. HIPAA also has ramifications for the workplace. In many church workplaces, we are accustomed to requesting prayers for employees and others who may be ill, hospitalized, or facing surgery. We are faith-based organizations and we may certainly continue to pray for our colleagues and clients when they face a health issue. However, we may only do so

1. "Facts about Sexual Harassment," accessed February 8, 2019, https://www.eeoc.gov/eeoc/publications/fs-sex.cfm.
2. Rosa Ehrenreich Brooks, "Dignity and Discrimination: Toward a Pluralistic Understanding of Workplace Harassment," *The Georgetown Law Journal* 88 (1999): 14–20.

after receiving permission from the person who is facing a health challenge and the information in the request for prayers should be worded without detail. Such caretaking respects the privacy and dignity of the person who is ill.

HIPPA also impacts questions we may or may not ask in an interview or on an application for employment. The Americans with Disabilities Act also places parameters around such questions. In the workplace, we must also protect the privacy of staff by restricting access to employee files that may contain Family and Medical Leave Act requests or any other private health information that may be contained in a file.

Conclusion

By way of review, employees are protected against discrimination due to the following:

- Age (treatment of those over the age of forty)
- Gender (usually interpreted as discrimination against women)
- Race, nationality, ethnic group, or color
- Disability

Because of all these protected classes, we hold the strong opinion that church employers need to think of themselves as just-cause employers rather than at-will employers. It is also the just and moral way to treat employees. Antidiscrimination laws are in place to correct long-standing and pervasive discrimination. As church employers, we should be at the forefront of standing against every kind of injustice and discrimination.

Other federal laws directly apply to workplace practices, and there are also many state and municipal laws concerning employment issues. For example, many states have already implemented minimum wage and personal leave laws that go beyond federal legislation. These laws are not treated in this book. Therefore we recommend that employers take steps to become aware and seek human resources and legal expertise to learn about situations covered by state and local municipal laws. Such legal implications may apply to many employment practices, particularly hiring, promoting, interviewing, compensating, and terminating staff.

When we think and act with justice in the workplace as our lynchpin, we make the church's mission to promote social justice a daily reality. Our religious values can help us avoid the legal pitfalls so prevalent in the American workplace.

In chapter 3, we examine the question of whether a church organization or faith community really needs personnel policies.

3

Do Faith Communities Need Personnel Policies?

Chapter Preview

As a follow-up to the previous chapter on "Civil and Legal Foundations," Fr. Dave will:

- Learn the rationale for personnel policies in the church workplace.
- Discover ways to develop and adopt personnel policies.
- Examine examples of appropriate content for personnel policies.

Introduction

Pastors and church administrators have questioned why human resources professionals are so insistent on policy development as a tool for good pastoral management of staff and volunteers. In some cases, because their organizations are small and informal, leaders believe they do not need to suffer the complications of developing and enforcing personnel policies. We hear pastors say, "We are a family here at St. Mary's Church and we don't need formal policies!" From time to time, however, in ways small or large, families go through periods of dysfunction.

Good personnel policies provide an excellent foundation for treating people fairly, equitably, and justly, especially in moments of stress or conflict. Sometimes families struggle to achieve "fairness," as siblings are quick to point out. Think of your own family of origin. Perhaps you're the oldest in your family and the other family members have biases and assumptions about what you will say or do, precisely because you are the oldest. The same family dynamics can happen in small parishes and church organizations because, over time, biases get woven into their very fabric.

GOOD PERSONNEL POLICIES PROVIDE AN EXCELLENT FOUNDATION FOR TREATING PEOPLE FAIRLY, EQUITABLY, AND JUSTLY, ESPECIALLY IN MOMENTS OF STRESS OR CONFLICT.

In a parish or church organization, the role of pastor, executive director, or administrator may be complicated by the realities of multiple relationships with the people on the staff. For example, the parish pastor may have a pastoral relationship, a personal relationship, and an employment relationship with staff members. Without written guidelines and policies, it can be difficult for him to act with consistency and fairness toward staff and volunteers. We will discuss multiplicity and complications of church employer relationships in other contexts as we look at human resources concerns, including the implications of multiple relationships in hiring, writing job descriptions, conducting performance evaluations, making compensation and benefits decisions, and that most difficult of issues, involuntary terminations.

Policy Development

Fortunately, pastors and directors have access to excellent resources for acquiring comprehensive personnel policies and adapting them to their parish or church organization. Roman Catholic dioceses usually provide excellent policy documents to parishes, schools, and agencies. Often dioceses provide written personnel policies that can be implemented at each site. Sometimes those policies are developed by diocesan staff and attorneys and promulgated as policy for all diocesan entities. Usually, however, dioceses provide written personnel policies for each parish, school, or agency, either for use as written or for adaptation by each entity. When parishes make adaptations, they should submit them to the diocese for review to ensure that specific personnel policies are reviewed for consistency and legal compliance. Just, equitable policies for the church workplace need to be consistent with civil law, clearly written and communicated to staffs, and fairly and consistently applied. Such policies provide the foundation for a just workplace environment.

JUST, EQUITABLE POLICIES FOR THE CHURCH WORKPLACE NEED TO BE CONSISTENT WITH CIVIL LAW, CLEARLY WRITTEN AND COMMUNICATED TO STAFFS, AND FAIRLY AND CONSISTENTLY APPLIED.

The policies of the workplace must comply with federal, state, and local law. The most obvious examples of such policies are those that deal with equal employment opportunity, that is, the absence of illegal discrimination in the workplace, payroll practices, overtime pay requirements, and family and medical leave policies. Employee handbooks are also a requirement, often met by publishing a handbook online for staff. The advantage of an online handbook is that policies can easily be updated and disseminated to staff. Policies that are not readily available to staff members in a paper or online format are not enforceable. Most employers require a signature form in each employee's file stating that he or she has received and read a copy of the policies or been given access to those policies online. Paper copies should be provided to any staff members without access to the online version.

Examples of Policies

What policies should be included in a church employment setting? We will provide a listing of some usual policies included in employee handbooks. We will also provide comments on any policies of particular interest in church settings. Essential policies often begin with statements about *work conditions*, *work settings*, and *work hours*. In schools, hospitals, and social service organizations, the hours and place where the work is to be performed are usually evident given the nature of the work. It's less obvious, however, in parishes and some other church organizations. These organizations should establish a normal workweek, while acknowledging that "normal" or "routine" is often difficult to define in a parish setting. Usually office staff will have regular hours, but pastoral staff persons are often called on to work evenings, weekends, and even holidays. Administration of work hours for pastoral staff needs to be managed by the pastor. A common issue arises when individuals on parish pastoral staffs want the freedom to work from home on occasion or to come into the office later than required in a normal workday schedule. These kinds of decisions need to be made by the pastor after consulting with the parish staff member who would like more flexible hours. Flexible hours in the parish are not helpful when the pastor doesn't know when people will be in the office, when he can schedule meetings, or how to encourage a sense of teamwork and collaboration if one or several of the pastoral staff members are not present on a predictable basis. Many parishes require their pastoral staff to be present before, during, or after Sunday liturgies. If there is a requirement that members of the pastoral staff be present on weekends, it is appropriate for those staff members to have a weekday off in the same way that the pastor takes a weekday off.

There are many other decisions that a pastor must make to manage work hours and insure staffing at the parish office. Another example of a common conflict is whether to require the regular presence of a parish musician in the office. When that musician is the director of liturgy, presence in the office during regular work hours may be required to encourage collaboration and teamwork.

Other essential policies address compensation and benefits protocols, vacation, sick leave, and other paid time off (PTO). These policies are often governed by diocesan policies or contracts with benefits providers. For example, compensation for teachers, principals, clergy, and vowed religious are often governed by diocesan policy. Civil law requires overtime compensation for nonexempt staff (see chapter 2). Eligibility for benefits is governed by the contracts the church organization executes with the benefits providers as well as by legislation such as the Affordable Care Act, Social Security, worker's compensation, and unemployment insurance. Sick leave benefits have been receiving increased attention by both federal legislative bodies as well as state entities. The federal government already mandates certain sick leave benefits under the Family and Medical Leave Act (FMLA). Whether a church organization, parish, or school is covered by FMLA is determined by the number of employees in each organization or by policy of the larger juridical umbrella covering the organization. For example, in a diocese whose corporate structure is that of *corporation sole*, the parishes and schools in that organization are likely to be required to follow the provisions of FMLA. It is particularly important to comply meticulously with all PTO policies. It is easy to be accused of discrimination if these policies are administered inconsistently. Employees need to have confidence that they are being treated equitably and fairly.

EMPLOYEES NEED TO HAVE CONFIDENCE THAT THEY ARE BEING TREATED EQUITABLY AND FAIRLY.

Employee handbooks normally include sections on *employee evaluation*, *promotion*, *professional growth and development*, and *supervision*. Employees have a right to receive formal feedback on their performance. How that feedback will be given is normally covered in policies. All organizations need policies on how they hire, terminate, conduct criminal background checks, implement child protection requirements, and handle employee behavior issues such as harassment and excessive absences. The policy should give assurance of nondiscrimination in all types of employee decision-making and the organization's commitment to diversity and justice in the church workplace. If the organization has a process—whether formal or informal—for bringing conflict or disagreements to resolution, the process should appear in the employee handbook.

EMPLOYEES HAVE A RIGHT TO RECEIVE FORMAL FEEDBACK ON THEIR PERFORMANCE.

Another issue is whether employees may bring their children into the workplace. If a child is ill or regular daycare is not available, it is rarely appropriate for the worker to bring that child to work. Children can be distracting and, if ill, possibly contagious. It would be better to have a *sick day* policy that allows parents to stay home with a sick child rather than bring the child to work and spread the illness to others.

There are other issues that regularly arise in a church workplace setting. *Conflicts of interest* are always a problem, especially in small organizations. Often one person in the organization selects vendors to supply goods or services. If that person has a conflict of interest with that vendor, such as a family relationship or friendship, the vendor decision will probably be biased and may not be in the organization's best interests. For example, a parish business manager's spouse runs a landscape business, so the landscaping contract moves to the spouse's company. Parishioners could become suspicious about that arrangement, especially if one of them also runs a landscaping business. This scenario begs the question as to whether preference should be given to businesses of parishioners in general. A wise colleague of mine with experience in matters of business ethics advises that donor relationships and business relationships are very different. We may run into all kinds of conflicts and questions when we confuse the nature of these relationships.

Another area requiring clear policies in a church organization such as a parish is that of *confidentiality*. Of course, the nature of pastoral relationships presumes confidentiality, the mandate for confidentiality being the highest for clergy in sacramental contexts, but also for pastoral staff members who provide counseling and pastoral care. Other settings require the highest levels of confidentiality, such as those dealing with parish and organizational records, and information about parishioner finances and donations. Even clerical staff in an office may have access to such information. Thus, it is incumbent on those with supervisory responsibility to have very clear, intentional, and explicit conversations with all staff members about the high standards of confidentiality that require adherence. School principals and staff may have access to family income and tax information by way of scholarship applications. A parish, school, or organization loses credibility whenever confidentiality is breached.

THE NATURE OF PASTORAL RELATIONSHIPS PRESUMES CONFIDENTIALITY, THE MANDATE FOR CONFIDENTIALITY BEING THE HIGHEST FOR CLERGY IN SACRAMENTAL CONTEXTS, BUT ALSO FOR PASTORAL STAFF MEMBERS WHO PROVIDE COUNSELING AND PASTORAL CARE.

Intellectual property may be an issue for a variety of church employees. Directors of religious education may have written materials and curriculum for catechetical programs. Church musicians often write music for their parish or organization. Who owns these materials? Written policies are needed to clarify copyright and publishing ownership. Most policies will say that if the writing was done while an employee of the parish and being compensated as such, these materials belong to the parish or organization. The discussion about these rights needs to happen in advance whenever possible. In such cases, a written agreement may specify joint ownership or individual ownership.

Perhaps the most sensitive and timely policy question is that of the requirement for *compliance with church teaching and behavioral norms*. Many if not most Catholic dioceses and parishes include such a policy as a requirement for all diocesan, parish, and school staff. It is based on these types of policies that churches resist the requirement of some legal entities to employ or provide benefits to those who do not meet the moral standards as applied by a church to which that organization belongs. For example, this policy has been used to deny benefits to same-sex couples or to refuse to recognize same-sex marriage. The standards iterated in these policies require all staff members to comply with the requirements of the policy, not just those who share that church's religious faith.

Other miscellaneous policies may be included in employee handbooks. These include the following:

- Dress standards
- Use of organization's property and supplies
- Outside employment
- Social media and other computer-related use
- Use of church vehicles
- Reimbursement for work-related transportation and other expenses

Many of the above policies also apply to volunteers. Normally, a separate volunteer policy document should be created. Churches are dependent on a large cadre of volunteers. They need to be aware of and understand what's expected of them.

> Good volunteer policies include statements regarding the following:
>
> - Recruitment and selection
> - Evaluation
> - Accountability
> - Child protection requirements
> - Terms of office
> - Use of church property
> - Termination, and
> - Expense reimbursement

The Leadership Roundtable (https://leadershiproundtable.org/) offers one of the most helpful tools available to parishes and church organizations. "The Catholic Standards for Excellence," a comprehensive set of best church management practices, provides Catholic entities with benchmarks by which to measure their human resource practices. Essential areas for employees, clergy, and volunteers, such as position descriptions, employee and volunteer reviews, orientations, and best practice policies are covered. The free program provides self-assessment tools to measure organizational practices against benchmarks and provides resources and templates to help implement practices and policies that require strengthening.

Conclusion

In Roman Catholic diocesan, parish, and school settings, policies are often promulgated under the umbrella of particular law and carry the weight of canon law.[1] This chapter has offered an overview of

1. Mary Santi, "Canon Law and Human Resources Policy Development," Keynote address to National Association of Church Personnel Administrators, Convocation at Greenville, South Carolina, April 21, 2015.

the kinds of policies crucial to creating workplaces and institutions that are just and on mission. The examples treated here do not exhaust the list of possible policies that may be needed. Nevertheless, daily implementation of carefully crafted and observed personnel routines go a long way toward building church organizations and parishes as places where staff persons feel they are treated fairly and equitably, and where everyone exercises accountability that fosters complementary aspirations and shared commitments.

In chapter 4, we will look at issues surrounding hiring, recruitment, and "onboarding."

4

Hiring

Finding the Right Person for the Right Position

Chapter Preview

In this chapter. Fr. Dave will:

- Learn why hiring well is a high priority for church organizations.
- Discover the importance of well-written and up-to-date job descriptions.
- Consider position analysis as a step in the hiring process.
- Investigate specific aspects of hiring, including the following:
  - Search committees
  - Search firms
  - Interviewing
  - Résumés and applications
  - References and credentials
  - Recruiting resources
- Consider orientation and probationary periods.

Introduction

Hiring well is a requirement for the success of a church organization. Finding the right people for positions in your organization is part science and part art. Hiring well establishes the basis for mission effectiveness, a pleasant and productive work culture, and avoidance of many difficult problems that arise when people are mismatched in employment settings. Hiring is the foundation for the effective administration of virtually all other functions of human resources and is as relevant for church workplaces as it is in for-profit corporations. It is also the foundation for ensuring justice and fair treatment of employees.

FINDING THE RIGHT PEOPLE FOR POSITIONS IN YOUR ORGANIZATION IS PART SCIENCE AND PART ART.

We cannot assume an employee knows what is expected of him or her if we do not provide a clear job description. We cannot accurately compare the value of one position to another without first having a full understanding of each position, nor can we determine the appropriate pay level for a position without analyzing its duties, responsibilities, accountabilities, and requirements. Likewise, we cannot evaluate an employee's performance if the employee has never been made aware of what is expected and how his or her performance will be evaluated. Much of what we will say about hiring the right employees also applies to recruiting and placing volunteers.

Where to Begin: Job Descriptions

You begin the hiring process long before you ever meet the first candidate. A successful search begins with careful planning and analysis. Step one is to determine the basics of the position for which you are hiring. If the position already exists, begin with the current job description. If there is no job description, get feedback from those who would best know the basic responsibilities and expectations: other staff and support persons, parishioners, even the person who previously held the position. This is an opportunity to build on and enhance the role and its fit with other staff members and their responsibilities. Are there other active roles in the parish or organization without written descriptions? If so, by building clear, interrelated job descriptions you can build deeper co-accountability and complementarity into the church workplace. We treat these opportunities at length below.

Job descriptions are used in several of the basic human resources functions of your organization. You will find them essential for recruiting and hiring. Job descriptions are also necessary for decisions about compensation, performance appraisal, succession planning, professional development, legal defense, reasonable accommodations as part of the Americans with Disabilities Act, and other aspects of organizational planning. We discuss them in this chapter on hiring, but well-crafted and up-to-date job descriptions will enhance all aspects of your organizational efforts. They are also very helpful in recruiting and retaining volunteers. Volunteer job descriptions are typically shorter and simpler to maintain and include abbreviated versions of the essentials in paid employee job descriptions.

WELL-CRAFTED AND UP-TO-DATE JOB DESCRIPTIONS WILL ENHANCE ALL ASPECTS OF YOUR ORGANIZATION.

What should an employee job description contain? Contents should include the following:

- Position title
- Exempt or nonexempt FLSA status
- Department within the organization if applicable
- Reporting structure, including supervisors and subordinates
- Summary of the position

- Responsibilities or tasks (those duties that occupy at least 5 percent of the employee's time)
- Essential intellectual and physical functions (including those listed for compliance with the Americans with Disabilities Act) as already mentioned in the chapter on "Civil and Legal Foundations"
- A statement that the list of duties is not exhaustive and may be changed
- A statement that the job description includes "other appropriate duties as required"

A pre-hiring job description sometimes states educational and experiential requirements and preferences for the position. These requirements and preferences may also be stated in recruiting documents. Design the job description as objectively as possible. It is not necessarily a description of the duties performed by the previous person who held this job. It is a description of the position duties and responsibilities that you need and are looking to fill.

If you don't have job descriptions for some or all on your staff, you can begin the process of developing those job descriptions by asking each person to write his or her own. Provide them with the template described above. We suggest that persons list any duty or responsibility on which they spend at least 5 percent of their time. They should conclude their job description with a final statement: "This job includes other appropriate duties as assigned." This will likely provoke lively discussion, so be ready. Every person on your staff needs to understand that flexibility is a requirement of the position. We may worry about staff members who balk at performing new or unassigned duties that aren't part of their job descriptions. This resistance may demonstrate lack of generosity or flexibility or even a lack of interest in the overall mission of the organization. Conversely, staff may worry that the statement is an invitation to supervisors to unfairly add new duties. Therefore, please note the word "appropriate" in the concluding statement. It is not appropriate to ask your administrative assistant to fix the boiler. But there are many times in the life of a parish, school, or other organization that require an adaptable staff member to take on an unusual yet nevertheless appropriate responsibility that matches his or her role and skill sets. Here is an opportunity to anticipate such occurrences and agree on the informal rules of problem solving and assignment.

MANY TIMES, AN ADAPTABLE STAFF MEMBER MIGHT BE ASKED TO TAKE ON AN UNUSUAL YET APPROPRIATE RESPONSIBILITY THAT MATCHES HIS OR HER ROLE AND SKILL SETS.

As staff members write their job descriptions, they need to understand that their statements do not actually become their job description until you as their supervisor, manager, pastor, or executive director confirm it. You are responsible to ensure roles are clear and are not redundant relative to others' roles. Likewise, you need to be sure that there are no gaps among the responsibilities named by your staff. You may even need to move duties and responsibilities one person has listed to another staff member. You may find that no one has taken on a crucial task. It is also your responsibility to be sure that tasks and responsibilities in a person's job description are closely matched to their strengths and talents. Nevertheless, we all end up with some responsibilities that align more with our limitations than with our strengths. Oversight requires both a critical eye and tolerance. Science meets art!

As each position description is written and reviewed, essential functions must be highlighted. Essential functions are those responsibilities essential to the purpose of the position. A person who cannot perform them, with or without a reasonable accommodation, can legally be denied employment in that position.

Job descriptions should be reviewed periodically with each individual employee by the pastor or supervisor. A natural time to do this is at the annual performance review. It is normal for job descriptions to continually evolve. A job description is a living document just as the organization is a living organization and change will be required. If planning and development happen in the parish or organization, priorities change and the expectations of staff members and volunteers change. If the job description is to be a helpful document in all aspects of human resources, then it needs to evolve as the priorities and responsibilities of the organization change. The introduction of a new hire poses real potential for change and realignment in most churches and small organizations.

An additional consideration: Sometimes, church employers decide to engage a person in their workplace under the title of "independent contractor." Often this does not meet the Internal Revenue Service's test that determines independent contractor status versus employee status. Employers are attracted to the use of independent contractors because these individuals do not have the same rights as employees, and employers do not have to provide benefits or pay the usual payroll taxes. However, there are serious penalties for misclassifying such individuals. Ordinarily, independent contractors, who are considered self-employed, are in business for themselves, provide services to several other organizations, and have primary control over what they do in their jobs. The Internal Revenue Service has posted guidelines to help you determine employee or independent contractor status. The more control an organization exercises over how, when, where, and by whom work is performed, the more likely the workers are employees, not independent contractors.

Independent Contractor or Employee?[1]

1. Behavioral: Does the company control or have the right to control what the worker does and how the worker does his or her job?
2. Financial: Are the business aspects of the worker's job controlled by the payer? (These include things like how worker is paid, whether expenses are reimbursed, who provides tools/supplies, etc.)
3. Type of Relationship: Are there written contracts or employee type benefits (e.g., pension plan, insurance, or vacation pay)? Will the relationship continue and is the work performed a key aspect of the business?

Position Analysis

In the hiring process, having a job description isn't enough to make good hiring decisions. A position analysis follows from development of the job description. It goes beyond a listing of duties and responsibilities for the position to include what it takes to successfully perform the work and describe who will succeed at it. The position analysis describes the qualities the successful candidate must possess. These qualities include knowledge, skills, abilities, personal traits, and experience.[2]

In many parishes and small Catholic agencies, knowledge and academic credentials may be undervalued. Sometimes the expertise required is overlooked in favor of strong personal qualities and relational skills. Consideration of personal traits is very important in church organizations, but not at the expense of the recognition that knowledge and academic credentials influence a person's ministerial

1. See https://www.irs.gov/businesses/small-businesses-self-employed/independent-contractor-self-employed-or-employee.

2. Edwin S. Mruk and William J. Yacullo, "Position Analysis: Executive Search for Catholic Organizations and the Key Ingredient for Success," *Whitepapers*, Trinity Executive Partnership website, 2. Accessible at http://www.trinityexecutivepartnership.com/white_papers.php.

or professional credibility. Most parishes and organizations can't afford to hire a person who requires a steep learning curve. An example of the importance of academic and experiential background is that of the lay ecclesial minister. The bishops of the United States clearly outline requirements for an effective layperson in ministry in their document *Co-Workers in the Vineyard of the Lord* (USCCB, 2005). Lay ministers need highly developed pastoral formation and skills as well as excellent academic preparation for their positions.

> Lay ecclesial ministers need
>
> - human qualities critical to form wholesome relationships and necessary to be apt instruments of God's love and compassion;
> - a spirituality and practice of prayer that root them in God's trinitarian life, grounding and animating all they do in ministry;
> - adequate knowledge in theological and pastoral studies, along with the intellectual skill to use it among the people and cultures of our country; and
> - the practical pastoral abilities called for in their particular ministry.[3]

Conversely, we often promote people into administrative positions who have wonderful technical and professional knowledge in their fields of ministry but no training in administration, leadership, finance, marketing, and human resources. We assume that the excellent catechist will also be an excellent director of religious education. Too often this is a formula for failure rather than success.

Relevant experience is also an important consideration in the selection process. However, the length of that experience may not be as significant as we might think. What is crucial is whether that experience has added significantly to the person's knowledge and abilities.

In addition to the specific skills needed for a position, such as writing, public speaking, or technological facility, leadership abilities determine one's potential for success in many of our positions. Can this person advance the mission and agenda of the organization? Does he or she have the communication and relational abilities to encourage others in the accomplishment of the mission? You are looking for personal traits that you believe are critical for the success of the person in this position. Be aware that often these personal characteristics may be different than your own. There are times when you do yourself a favor by hiring someone who is very different from you, and who enjoys and excels at different tasks than those in your own areas of expertise.

At the same time, you must be realistic about the kind of staff member you can hire given your compensation and benefits limitations. Sometimes, to save costs, employers decide to hire only part-time staff who are not eligible for benefits. However, this may result in an inability to attract competent people for your vacant positions.

If you are the appointing officer or will be the person's direct supervisor, you must hire with the right "fit" in mind. The interview process will be a primary means of discerning the right fit.

Recruiting

We're often asked whether we need to advertise all job openings even if we already know who will fill the position. There is no clear answer. Some dioceses and organizations have policies that require

3. USCCB, *Co-Workers in the Vineyard of the Lord*, 34.

at least an internal posting of all positions. In that case, you must do the internal posting. You might be pleasantly surprised by who applies for the position. It may be someone more qualified than the person you planned to hire or promote. Sometimes you might want to advertise a position even though you are leaning toward promoting someone from within. You may even find that a review of applicants confirms this. However, it is also possible that you will find a better candidate by posting both internally and externally. But if your decision to promote from within is firm, then it is not always necessary to advertise for that position. When a decision has been made, it doesn't make sense to use resources for a pro forma search.

Recruitment methodologies include resources available within the organization such as internal posting, newsletters, parish bulletins, and organizational websites. Print media and university recruiting are excellent external tools. On the internet, there are myriad options for posting job openings to invite quick and appropriate responses. Some internet recruitment resources used by church employers include Catholicjobs.com, Monster.com, Ziprecruiter.com, and Indeed.com.

Print media remains a viable option even in our high-tech society. It is important to use print media in a way that reaches large numbers of people. For example, advertising in a Spanish-language newspaper can provide candidates who are bilingual and will be able to function effectively in a bilingual parish. Eliciting a diverse pool of candidates is an important goal of effective job-marketing. As a fundamental aspect of recruiting, we strive to avoid perceptions of discrimination built into the selection process. All recruiting methods need to avoid wording that signals discrimination. Poor wording of an advertisement could hold clues to a discriminatory attitude. For example, if you say you are looking for an "energetic and technology savvy candidate," you are indicating a preference for someone young rather than an openness to a qualified person of any age. You are also indicating that people with disabilities are not welcome even in a situation where the disability would not prohibit the ability to fulfill the essential functions of the position. Where and how we advertise is part of how we avoid even the appearance of discrimination. In a widely focused job marketing process, we show our willingness to discover candidates from diverse backgrounds who can capably fulfill the functions of this position. If the candidate's religious preference is a requirement for the job, you can state this in the advertisement without risking a charge of discrimination, as church employers may discriminate based on religion. All recruiting written materials should include the statement that the organization is an equal employment opportunity employer.

Search Committees

Using a group of people from your workplace to assist in the hiring process can be very effective. The use of search committees has increased in recent decades. Such committees foster a sense of collegiality as well as provide a range of impressions and opinions that can significantly assist the hiring agent. The use of search committees reflects a commonsense notion that in evaluating talent, several brains are better than one. Such committees normally have five or six members who have knowledge of the organization as well as good judgment. A search committee is usually appropriate for a position that has professional or ministerial significance in the organization. In parishes, such committees are often used when searching for ministerial positions, business managers, and development directors.

Search committees may be helpful at the very outset of the hiring process in the position analysis tasks described earlier. Committee members most likely make a real contribution to a description of a successful applicant. Well-chosen committee members are familiar with the workplace culture, the organization's mission, and its internal and community culture. In a widely representative committee, each member shares both common and unique perspectives at different stages in the hiring process.

Some might be too quickly enamored with the first candidate who is interviewed. In contrast, others might observe off-putting as well as attractive qualities in each of the applicants. Effective search-committee members provide balance in perspectives to the process of matching persons with expectations and job responsibilities.

Search Firms and Consultants

Although it is unusual for small organizations, schools, or parishes to use professional search firms or consultants, sometimes using a professional firm can be very helpful and worth the cost. Some executive or specialized positions make finding the right person more difficult, so engaging a consultant may increase the likelihood of successfully finding and selecting candidates. Positions that are sometimes better filled with the assistance of a search firm or consultant include executive directors of organizations, school principals, and directors of development or marketing. The fees for such searches are usually a percentage, about one-third, of the annual salary for the position, plus expenses.

Interviewing

Interviews are critical to successful hiring. In the interview, an attractive candidate is invited and encouraged to consider a position in the organization. At the same time, the interview provides the opportunity to get to know a candidate, evaluate qualifications, and decide on fit and appropriateness for the organization. Sometimes initial screening interviews are conducted via telephone or Skype, but nothing can replace the face-to-face interview before a final decision is made. There may be more than one interview, though ordinarily there is only one interview with the search committee. This interview may be preceded or followed by individual interviews with committee members, members of the staff, and, of course, the designated leader or supervisor. I recommend thorough preparation of the committee members regarding the applicant's résumé, qualifications, and references. Preparation includes decisions about the specific interview questions and who will ask those questions. The committee is not limited to prearranged questions but should cover all significant inquiries for the sake of thoroughness and comparison.

As a crucial matter of preparation, educate each person conducting interviews about appropriate and inappropriate questions. Inappropriate or illegal questions include the following:

- Applicant's age or year of high school graduation
- Marital status
- Family planning and childcare issues
- Number of arrests
- Disabilities or anything related to matters of health or physical well-being
- Military service discharge status
- Economic status
- Sexual orientation
- Race or nationality
- Height or weight

The organization may be accused of illegal discrimination if an interviewee is asked questions in these areas, particularly when the person is not hired.

What types of questions *should* you ask? Make inquiries that

- Are knowledge or skills related;
- Allow the candidate to share his or her personality and motivation;
- Relate to the job description; and
- Relate to the organization for which you are hiring, including values and ecclesiology, especially when looking to fill ministerial positions.

Effective interviews include questions such as, "Tell me about a time when you worked on a project with others and that project was successful," or, "Tell me about a time when you worked on a project that failed." Both are behavioral interview questions and both questions should be asked. You are looking at past behaviors that predict successful employment in your organization. Do not be concerned when an applicant tells you about something that didn't work. The important part of that narrative discloses whether the applicant tries new things and learns from successes as well as failures. We are more worried about the person who can't relate a failure to the interviewer. Does that mean he or she has never tried anything or taken a risk? Failure is not a problem. Lack of learning or problem solving in the face of a failure is a problem.

DO NOT BE CONCERNED WHEN AN APPLICANT TELLS YOU ABOUT SOMETHING THAT DIDN'T WORK....FAILURE IS NOT A PROBLEM. LACK OF LEARNING OR PROBLEM SOLVING IN THE FACE OF A FAILURE IS A PROBLEM.

Hypothetical interview questions are also excellent ways to get to know an applicant's leadership style and problem-solving ability. You can make up a situation or recall one that is appropriate to the position you are seeking to fill and ask how the applicant might solve or address the situation. For example, "What would you do, if in your new role as school principal, you discovered that a group of parents who have not accepted the departure of the former principal, seem determined to undermine your efforts and thwart your success?" This is a far more effective question than, "Tell me about your leadership style."

Finally, it is always a good idea to end the interview by inviting the candidate to ask questions or voice concerns.

References and Credentials

It is necessary to verify credentials in today's culture of exaggerating qualifications such as academic achievement. Do not assume that the information on the résumé is true. Call or contact universities or other institutions of higher learning such as trade schools or technology institutes to verify an applicant's credentials. There may be a small fee to get the information, but it is worth it. Ordinarily, they will tell you only the degree or certificate that was earned and the date that it was awarded. If you want transcripts, they must be requested *by the applicant* and sent to you.

You must also check references. These include the ones provided by the applicant, but you are not restricted only to those provided. You may call anyone whom you think might be helpful. However, it is better not to call a current employer or coworker until the applicant gives you permission. The applicant may not yet have told them of his or her plans to look for another position. Some references might not answer your questions because they have concerns about liability for a negative recommendation. Such organizations might have a policy to share only basic information, such as position title and dates of tenure. However, that does not prevent you from asking for a recommendation. Ordinarily, you will assure the person giving the information of confidentiality.

Résumés, Applications, and Employee Files

Most applicants will submit a résumé and cover letter to begin their side of the application process. The employer responds with a summary of the job responsibilities and requirements and requests the completion of the standard application form in use by the organization. Standard application forms have several advantages over résumés. The information they elicit will be more standardized. Typical queries might include previous work experience with month and date of hire and month and date of termination, and reason for leaving the position. Such information is not always provided on a résumé, thus leaving the possibility of unaccounted months or even years of work experience.

As a prospective employer, you have a right to information about gaps in employment and reasons for a person leaving a position. Gaps in employment are usually understandable but should not be hidden in a résumé. Likewise, there can be excellent reasons for leaving a position, but you as the employer have a right to inquire about those reasons. The application form includes information that may appear on some but not all submitted applications and résumés, about academic institutions attended, dates of attendance, major and minor areas of study, and dates of receiving degrees or certificates. However, high school graduation dates cannot be requested because it may be viewed to engage in age discrimination.

The application form should include a statement informing applicants that any material misrepresentation discovered on the application, in the résumé, or during the interviewing and hiring process, will result in disqualification from the hiring process or, after a hiring, dismissal. There is no time limit on this consequence for misrepresentation. If you cannot trust the person's responses or representations during hiring, the person cannot be trusted as an employee.

Applicant files are opened when a résumé or application is submitted to the employer. The applicant file becomes the employee file if the person is hired. If a candidate is not hired, the applicant file should be retained for three years in case of litigation. Each candidate should be sent a letter as soon as you are certain that he or she is no longer being considered for the position. Ordinarily, these letters are sent when an offer of employment has been accepted by the chosen candidate. You need not give detailed reasons for rejection. It is enough to thank the person for applying and share that a person who best fit the requirements and preferences for the position has been offered the job. This letter is to be retained in the applicant file.

The employee file is opened when the person is offered and accepts the position. Employee files continue to be added to through the tenure of each person in the organization. Employee files include the following:

- Application
- Résumé
- Employment and academic credential verifications
- Criminal background check results

- Current and past job descriptions
- Contact information
- Performance reviews
- Compensation reviews
- Benefits' elections
- Disciplinary memos
- Commendations
- I-9 form[4]
- State and federal W-4 forms
- Personal data such as address, phone, personal e-mail, etc.
- Documentation of continuing education
- Documentation of professional growth and use of professional growth allowance if the employer has such a provision
- Attendance records, including use of vacation days, sick days, family and medical leave, personal leaves, and miscellaneous paid time off[5]
- Letter of resignation
- Notification of discharge
- Exit interview
- Any other documents pertaining to the continuing retention or the discharge of the employee

Orientation and Probation Periods

All new staff members need orientation, also known as *onboarding*. Orientation is important for all levels of staff as this is the opportunity to explain how things work, the roles of colleagues and other staff members, and describe or introduce key leadership in the organization such as parish council members, school board, board of directors, clients, and other key volunteers. The higher the position in the parish or organization, the deeper and longer the orientation should be. An effective orientation process includes easy access to leadership and colleagues who can answer questions and explain the protocols and dynamics of the organization. For key leaders, including new pastors and new executive directors, support and feedback can last as long as two years. It often takes at least a year for some significant questions and issues to emerge.

As new staff members begin employment, probation periods of three to six months keep both employer and employee in productive communication. Mutual feedback during this time allows timely recognition of performance problems or structures that might be frustrating success or find ways to turn a small achievement into a larger implementation. With immediate feedback, it is often possible to correct a problem before it grows into something that interferes with mission effectiveness. Probation periods also give the new employee a chance to evaluate his or her role in the organization. The new

4. Most employers keep work eligibility documentation in a separate file with the documents of all other employees in case of a federal audit.

5. It is good practice to keep any records of information related to an employee's health held separately and given special protections of confidentiality, in a secure place such as a locked file cabinet.

employee may realize that this new position is not a good fit, and he or she would like to make a change quickly and without judgment.

Probation periods also facilitate easier partings when the person and the job are just not a good fit. Termination during probation rarely results in legal action or the kinds of difficulties that ensue when termination takes place after a longer period of employment. While you can never terminate an employee during a probation period for discriminatory reasons, termination is the right action if the employee is not performing well or does not fit in well in the organization. Sometimes, the problem is so serious that termination is the best solution. When a new person isn't doing well but is not told of problems quickly, silence and tolerance serve neither the person nor the mission. Instead, months, even years go by, and it becomes too difficult to take appropriate action. Either the feedback comes too late to bring about change, or the problem settles into the system, not rising to the level of termination but continuing to manifest itself in the workplace.

Conclusion

Anyone who has been in leadership can tell you about the successes and difficulties he or she experienced in hiring. Most will advise you not to settle for someone whom you hope works out but about whom you have serious doubts. The process may take longer than you had anticipated. If you have not found the right person and you are up against a deadline, look for an interim solution rather than settling for the person about whom you have serious doubts.

One of the most important responsibilities of a pastor or church organization leader is developing skilled, co-accountable staff persons who work together to implement the mission, goals, and objectives of the parish or organization. It is a challenging responsibility that, when done well, yields enormous returns.

In chapter 5, we will look at the elements of a healthy workplace, the importance of conflict management, and the importance of good communication and well-planned meetings.

5

The Ongoing Employment Relationship

Chapter Preview

In this chapter, Fr. Dave will:

- Examine strengths-based leadership as a tool for management and engagement.
- Consider elements of a healthy church workplace.
- Learn the importance of conflict management.
- Review the centrality of excellent communication and well-planned meetings.

Introduction

You, as a church leader, can create a healthy and thriving ministry setting with consistent communication, coaching, directing, and mentoring of your staff. Sometimes a pastor might say he doesn't like spending the time it takes to create a well-functioning and effective staff. He would rather spend his time *doing ministry*. I am convinced that a pastoral leader does great ministry when he or she fosters ministerial effectiveness among the whole team. The leader's delegation multiplies ministry effectiveness by the number of people who have been empowered to do ministry well and do ministry together.

THE EFFECTIVE PASTORAL LEADER CONSISTENTLY BUILDS STRONG RELATIONSHIPS WITH STAFF AND VOLUNTEERS, IN ADDITION TO PARISHIONERS OR CLIENTS

You need to learn the key human resources hiring concepts and the basics about compensation, transitions, performance reviews, and legal issues. Effective and even exciting achievement of mission happens in the day-to-day workings of the organization and in the ordinary routine of leading staff and volunteers. At the heart of the leadership function, the effective pastoral leader consistently builds strong relationships with staff and volunteers, in addition to parishioners or clients.

Strengths-Based Leadership and Engagement

Have you ever worked with a positive leader, one who builds trust, communicates belief in the mission, and believes in your ability to contribute to that mission? How was that experience for you? Bring that person to mind and reflect on your experience. You have probably also experienced a leader whose style is based on criticism, micromanagement, lack of trust, and fear. What was that experience like? Was it effective in the short term? In the long term?

The designated leader's role in an organization builds an effective team of staff and volunteers, fosters excellent relationships with other team members, models excellent communication, provides development opportunities for each person on the team, and inspires effective mission implementation. The positive leader has the best chance to succeed at these lofty and important tasks. He or she always looks for ways to build trust and nurture compassion as basic elements of workplace culture, to foster stability, and, more than anything else, to foster hope even in the face of great obstacles and constraints.[1] The negative leader is a pessimist who expects failure and is overwhelmed by obstacles. As leaders in faith-based organizations, we convey hope, not only in the reign of God, but also in the immediate experience of hope that believes we will find ways to succeed even in the face of immediate crises and long-term difficulties. Consistent with that intent, many church organizations implement planning processes based on a methodology called "appreciative inquiry," fundamentally based on looking at corporate strengths and building on those qualities throughout the organization.[2]

Many believe that if we work on weaknesses, we will fix ourselves or our organizations. This myth suggests that if all weaknesses are corrected, excellence will be achieved. We are most likely to achieve excellence, in ourselves and our organizations, by focusing on and developing our strengths. We need to "focus on strengths and manage the weaknesses."[3] Research from the Gallup Corporation, a leader in promoting strengths-based leadership, clearly indicates that time spent developing strengths is far more effective and successful than time spent fixing weaknesses. You don't learn about excellence by studying failure. When individuals know their strengths, they are empowered to make tangible contributions to their organizations, and their engagement in that organization is enhanced.

YOU DON'T LEARN ABOUT EXCELLENCE BY STUDYING FAILURE.

The Clifton "StrengthsFinder" Profile is the preferred tool used to help people identify and understand their strengths. It is used as a resource for worker engagement in for-profit, nonprofit, and church organizations. Over 15 million people across several nations and cultures have used this tool. The StrengthsFinder Profile is accessed through the Gallup organization's website or by means of a code provided in several of the Gallup books about the StrengthsFinder tool (see Rath and Conchie). Addressing managers, a speaker at the Gallup Workplace Engagement Workshop held in Chicago on December 7, 2016, observed, "70% of your payroll goes to people who aren't engaged in their job." People whose work draws on their strengths rather than their weaknesses are more engaged in their work. However, naming everyone's strengths is no Pollyanna endeavor. While no one escapes from occasionally taking on tasks that engage a weakness, by naming our strengths, we are in a better position to recognize when we are being stretched. Of course, minimizing such work is helpful to the whole organization.

1. Tom Rath and Barry Conchie, *Strengths Based Leadership: Great Leaders, Teams, and Why People Follow* (New York: Gallup Press, 2009), 1–3.

2. See, e.g., Susan Paddock, *Appreciative Inquiry in the Catholic Church* (Plano, TX: Think Book, 2003).

3. Donald O. Clifton and Paula Nelson, *Soar with Your Strengths: A Simple Yet Revolutionary Philosophy of Business and Management* (New York: Bantam Books, 1995), 18.

When persons take on responsibilities based on their strengths, they maximize effectiveness of organizations, committees, councils, or work teams.

PEOPLE WHOSE WORK DRAWS ON THEIR STRENGTHS RATHER THAN THEIR WEAKNESSES ARE MORE ENGAGED IN THEIR WORK.

Effective leaders engage staffs to eliminate work silos—situations where people are kept apart, or even keep themselves isolated—and foster collaboration. You may find the Clifton StrengthsFinder very helpful in this. When you promote collaboration, you increase the likelihood that the person with the strengths for a project will be the one who leads or implements the project. We have all had the experience of working with someone who has a great idea, but if asked to implement the idea, fails. Execution of a project requires a very different set of strengths than having the initial idea does. It is easy to confuse those skills. Creating partnerships and teams around strengths builds effective pastoral or organizational leadership. When you invite people to do what they do best, success is far more likely.

Mission effectiveness and focus are dramatically and positively affected when the language of strengths is normalized in your workplace. With the proper mindset, you will notice many more opportunities to build on the talents of your staff and volunteers. You will also find that the use of strengths language is especially potent in managing volunteers. When you or your staff recognize that a volunteer needs to be moved out of a position, search out or create a position where his or her strengths will be more fully utilized. The effort is far more affirming to a volunteer and, moreover, witnesses to others that you respect and value volunteers as significant contributors to the work and mission.

Many parishes use the Clifton StrengthsFinder as a tool for parishioner engagement. When the staff is already comfortable with the language and processes of the Clifton StrengthsFinder, the parish will be effectively served by use of the same tool.

The Healthy Church Workplace

Parker Palmer once said, "A leader is a person who holds an unusual degree of power to project on other people his or her shadow or his or light."[4] Positive staff relationships are the key ingredients in a healthy, productive church workplace. Critically important are the one-to-one relationships between you as the leader and each individual staff member. You set the tone for the times when you meet or collaborate with the staff. As the pastor or leader, you have incredible influence to shape the mission and empower the culture with love and effectiveness.

When employees resign from a position, they often tell you that it is for more money or better benefits, but the most common reason for leaving a job is strained relationships—with the supervisor or with other members of the staff. Most employers put a high value on staff retention for financial reasons and mission effectiveness. Building positive workplace relationships is key to retaining staff. Opportunities for talented employees are growing and they are being tempted away for a variety of reasons. We have witnessed this trend in Catholic schools for several years. The baby boomer teachers are retiring, and it is increasingly difficult to find replacements for experienced teachers in both public and private schools. This phenomenon also occurs in church organizations and parishes. High turnover comes with high replacement costs but even higher costs in effectiveness and donations to the organization.

4. Parker J. Palmer, *Let Your Life Speak: Listening to the Voice of Vocation* (San Francisco: Jossey-Bass, 1999).

Parishioners are generous when their needs are being met and they are being served well. Benefactors support organizations they perceive as stable and on mission.

Building relationships among staff and volunteers is a primary function of the leader in developing the healthy church workplace. As you know your staff, appreciate and use their gifts, provide opportunities for professional development and participation in meaningful ministries and projects, they will respond by being engaged in the organization and working hard toward the accomplishment of the goals and mission of the organization. The human resources director at Mercy Home for Boys and Girls once observed, "We try to make sure that everyone prides themselves on the mission, that they're feeling supported and that they're getting what they need." Engagement and retention are partners in an effective workplace.

Coaching, directing, and communicating with team members are the ordinary means of creating a positive culture for ministry and performance effectiveness. Encouragement of each staff member comes first. You need to pay attention, notice details, notice small jobs well done, and, of course, motivate toward big picture success. Your motivation makes all the difference. At the same time, you also need to notice the small problems, difficulties, and obstacles. Help employees come up with their own solutions to those issues and lean toward suggesting solutions only as a fallback remedy.

Sometimes, ordinary communication includes confronting a problem caused or not effectively handle by one of your staff members. It is best to have a private and immediate conversation with that person to address the issue. Perhaps the issue is failure to meet a deadline, lack of presence at an event or a meeting, absenteeism, or a poorly handled confrontation or conversation. Such problems are best treated in the ordinary supervisory process, thus avoiding the drama and difficulty of a major confrontation. You will find that most of your coaching and supervising will be positive encounters that, in turn, create a positive environment and make corrective conversations less difficult.

Coaching helps people reach professional results and become self-starters. Taking initiative doesn't happen in an organizational culture dominated by fear but in one focused on teaching and encouragement. Do people on your staff take responsibility, not only for their own duties, but for the effectiveness of the whole parish or organization? When you are coaching, you are primarily motivating good performance and advancing professional development. Part of your role as a coach is to give performance feedback, both formally and informally, in the periodic performance review.

Mentoring is a more intense process for the pastoral leader and is not a requirement for designated leaders. However, you will probably have an opportunity to work with young people in ministry or people moving from secular positions to church positions who need some extra attention to make the transition. Coaching and mentoring in these situations may seem interchangeable, but mentoring is a long-term commitment and has a long-term goal of developing the person. Mentoring isn't limited to supervisor/staff relationships. You are likely to be asked for mentoring from people whom you do not supervise but who are looking for guidance and professional development from a proven church leader. When accepting such invitations, you too may learn and your leadership skills may improve. However, in a workplace setting, the goal of mentoring is to help the person grow and gain greater competence and maturity. It is focused on developing qualities and targeting behaviors that make the person more effective in their job or ministry.[5]

If you are the pastor of a parish, you may be fortunate enough to be a mentor to a newly ordained priest or clergy member. This is an exceptional role and one with major implications for the future of the church. Clergy and others on a staff may also mentor a young member of the clergy as he prepares for his next assignment, and these days that often means assignment as a pastor.

5. Two helpful guides to these practices are Marty Brounstein, *Coaching and Mentoring for Dummies* (Foster City, CA: IDG Books, 2000); and several pages at the Exforsys.com consulting organization's training website, accessed February 8, 2019, http://www.exforsys.com/career-center/coaching-mentoring.html.

Mentoring requires a skill set like that required of anyone who is an effective minister. As a mentor, you need excellent relationship-building skills. You need good listening, questioning, and communication skills. You will help those you mentor to develop goals and action plans, and to develop the ability to measure and test the success of their implementations. It is important that you help the person you mentor to be realistic and take initiative in place of dependency on you, the mentor. Perhaps the most important personal asset of all is a healthy sense of humor.

Managing Conflict

How do you handle conflict in your organization, on your staff, or in other workplace settings? Directly addressing conflict in a church setting is difficult and often is avoided by people in ministry. But conflict should not be avoided, because on a well-functioning team there are important periods of testing that rise to the point of conflict. It is often an essential step in coming to the best decisions and solutions as we strategically plan, act, and evaluate. Patrick Lencioni is founder and president of a top management consulting firm that specializes in organizational health and executive team development. Mr. Lencioni addresses the important role of healthy conflict. Here is how he defines conflict:

> Of course, the kind of conflict I am referring to here is not the nasty kind that centers around people or personalities. Rather, it is what I call productive ideological conflict, the willingness to disagree, even passionately when necessary, around important issues and decisions that must be made. But this can only happen when there is trust. When there is trust, conflict becomes nothing but the pursuit of truth, an attempt to find the best possible answer.[6]

When church staffs and leadership teams avoid the discomfort of conflict, they can pass that discomfort on to their constituents or parishioners. They fail to arrive at the most creative and effective decision available to them. Lencioni describes a "Conflict Continuum" that goes from artificial harmony to a conflict point to a destructive, mean-spirited personal attack.[7]

Conflicts, difficulties, and disagreements are normal and not to be feared. Conflict can lead to creativity and positive change and is not to be avoided to feign agreement or consensus when it doesn't exist. Conflicts will happen among colleagues, subordinates, staff, and parishioners. Look for the ways the conflict can take you and your organization to greater effectiveness. However, sometimes conflict simmers and boils over, becoming destructive.

What are some of the causes of conflict in the church setting? Pastors and supervisors can cause conflict by micromanaging or, at the opposite extreme, by abdicating decision-making. You, as designated leader, may appear to be taking sides, being dismissive, overreacting, or in other ways dividing your team. Perhaps your expectations are not clearly defined. Perhaps you have rescued instead of coaching through a problem situation. Often, the conflict is between colleagues. Your first strategy as the designated leader is to empower your colleagues and communicate that you expect them to handle the conflict themselves and seek help from you when they agree they cannot resolve it. In some situations, you may help them seek a skilled mediator. Nevertheless, you may be called on to be a mediator among staff members. To be an effective mediator, you must establish ground rules for the mediation meeting, be an active listener, work to identify areas of resistance, and negotiate possible solutions while not becoming a one-person judge and jury, or worse, a parent.

6. Patrick Lencioni, *The Advantage: Why Organizational Health Trumps Everything Else in Business* (San Francisco: Jossey-Bass, 2012), 38.
7. Lencioni, *The Advantage*, 42.

Conflict between yourself and someone whom you supervise is not uncommon. Conflicts may be about communication, work habits, attitude, or even insubordination. As a designated leader, it is important that you be honest about your role in the conflict. Set a goal for the meeting that helps you both get back on track. Accept that you can only control your own responses, perspective, expectations, and energy. Don't be afraid to handle the conflict. The results will be worth it.

There is help available to you as you approach conflict management in your organization. One of the most current and focused perspectives on how we handle disagreements in ministry is offered by Ann Garrido in her pastorally sensitive book *Redeeming Conflict*. She says, "The first responsibility of the Christian community—whether it be expressed in the form of a parish congregation, university, hospital, group of vowed religious, social service agency, etc.—is to deepen its members' capacities and skills for friendship, and that includes the ability to manage disagreements well."[8] Dr. Garrido discusses twelve practices for living and serving amid diverse backgrounds, perspectives, and behaviors. She discusses effective communication skills, the role of emotion, self-awareness, forgiveness, and problem solving. These practices could be excellent fodder for staff meetings and as tools for ministerial development.

Meetings

Most of this chapter has focused on the many ways excellent communication creates a productive and healthy workplace. Many, if not most difficulties in the employment setting are either abrogated or avoided by the leader's continued focus on fostering excellent communication throughout the organization. Well-planned and effective meetings are primary ways to enhance communication.

Are you one of the many people who hear the word *meeting* and groan? How many meetings have we planned or participated in that were a waste of time and effort? Patrick Lencioni, in his classic bestseller *Death by Meeting* (2004), admits to being a big supporter of *good* meetings, but he rails against bad meetings.[9] He observes that the main problem with meetings is that we try to cover every possible topic at once—in what we call a *staff meeting*. In the name of efficiency, we put strategic issues, immediate concerns, and long-term planning into the same meeting. This doesn't work. We might need *more* meetings—more effective meetings.

The time spent planning and conducting well-designed meetings will be well worth it. Most administrative issues, as well as the tactical concerns that rightly occupy most meetings, can be handled efficiently and quickly. Strategy meetings are less frequent and can be productive if everyone is thinking in a strategic context, rather than trying to deal with other kinds of agenda items. Lencioni asserts that healthy and effective organizations have healthy and effective meetings, where real work gets done and participants are not bored or passive. Good meetings result in the empowerment of others to fully engage in all the aspects of ministry and mission of the parish, school, or organization. Accountability becomes real, so that persons on the ministry team learn they can trust and rely on each other. Good meetings work![10]

8. Ann Garrido, *Redeeming Conflict: 12 Habits for Christian Leaders* (Notre Dame, IN: Ave Maria Press, 2016), 6–7.

9. Patrick Lencioni, *Death by Meeting: A Leadership Fable...about Solving the Most Painful Problem in Business* (San Francisco: Jossey-Bass, 2004).

10. See also Lencioni, *The Advantage*, 173–87.

Chapter Summary

When you pay attention to the culture, relationships, and excellence in ordinary communication, you will come to your office excited to take on the next project and confident that you are doing God's work in your church or mission-centered organization.

In chapter 6, we will examine performance management, and how to use tools such as reasonable expectations, informal feedback, and formal reviews.

6

Performance Management

The Responsibility of Every Leader

Chapter Preview

In this chapter, Fr. Dave will:

- Recognize performance management as an important set of tools for achieving organizational and individual excellence.
- Examine reasonable expectations of staff and volunteers.
- Learn the importance of informal feedback in performance management.
- Assess formal appraisal processes, including
    - ♦ Performance appraisal tools and methodology; and
    - ♦ Common errors in the appraisal process.

Managing for Excellence

As someone responsible for an organization, school, or church, your leadership includes ensuring that the mission is well implemented and holding people accountable for their roles in that implementation. When we identify accountability and performance assessment as normative contributions of effective leaders, some might say that we are adopting a business or secular model of management. My own perspective, as a person with a long history in church ministry and leadership, says that since no organization can claim a more consequential mission, we therefore must also set the highest standards for ourselves and others as we evaluate and nurture both individual and group performance. As a church leader, you are responsible for providing feedback to staff members, whether paid or volunteer. I will use parish life and ministry as the primary focus in this chapter, but the concepts are equally applicable to all church-related organizations.

THE MISSION OF CHURCH ORGANIZATIONS IS SO CONSEQUENTIAL THAT WE MUST SET THE HIGHEST STANDARDS FOR OURSELVES AND OTHERS AS WE EVALUATE AND NURTURE BOTH INDIVIDUAL AND GROUP PERFORMANCE.

Pope Francis describes the parish as

> the environment for hearing God's word, for growth in the Christian life, for dialogue, proclamation, charitable outreach, worship and celebration. In all its activities, the Parish encourages and trains its members to be evangelizers. It is a community of communities, a sanctuary where the thirsty come to drink in the midst of their journey, and a center of constant missionary outreach. (*Evangelii Gaudium* 28)

Parishes and other church organizations are charged with a mission that is unequaled by any other. With that charge comes the responsibility of implementing mission as fully and effectively as possible. As lofty and divine as that mission is, ordinary humans do the day-to-day work of implementation.

Some may consider performance management and performance appraisal as practically identical, but they are mistaken. Performance management is a broader concept and includes analysis of the organization's implementation of its vision and plan. It is strategic and key to the role of parish councils, boards of directors, and executive leadership. Performance appraisals are the tools with which supervisors examine the roles and performance of individuals in the accomplishment of their specific goals and objectives toward implementation of the organization's plans.

Reasonable Expectations of Staff and Volunteers

Effective mission implementation begins with good communication and planning. Does each person understand the mission? Does each person know what is expected of him or herself? Have expectations been clearly communicated to everyone? Does each person know that he or she will be evaluated on meeting those expectations?

The National Association of Church Personnel Administrators published a position paper entitled "The Individual and the Institution." This publication highlights several expectations that church employers ought to have of their employees. Employees should

- Complete assigned duties in a timely fashion;
- Adhere to reasonable rules of workplace conduct;
- Be honest and exercise care in the use of institutional materials, resources and property;
- Show cooperation, commitment, and flexibility beyond the normal workplace duties for the sake of mission;
- Respect the employer's hiring processes and decisions when such processes are nondiscriminatory and consistently applied;
- Respect the institution's policies and procedures to achieve its mission;
- Alert supervisors to organizational problems;
- Understand, accept, and contribute to the mission with commitment, initiative, and responsibility;
- Interact with others with dignity, cooperation, and respect; and
- Consistently work toward the creation of healthy working relationships in the organization by participation, cooperation, flexibility, and valuing of diversity.[1]

1. National Association of Church Personnel Administrators (NACPA), "The Individual and the Institution: Strengthening Working Relationships in the Church" (Third Position Paper of NACPA, 1994), 18–20.

This list is not exhaustive. Moreover, in order to be helpful to any specific church organization, expectations must be written and communicated using the language and specifics of the organization's culture and mission. However, the list illustrates the broad range of expectations for accountability. We affirm and respect people when we hold them to high standards and then communicate that we believe they can meet those standards. Sometimes leaders of church organizations, particularly pastors, believe that holding people accountable is not "pastoral." Giving negative feedback is difficult, but it also provides the opportunity to communicate clearly that the mission is why we are here. In thorough performance reviews, negative feedback is not all that is communicated. Both tone and manner of feedback matter. Communicating positive assessments helps an employee understand what is going right, and that such performance really matters to the mission. Fundamentally, if we believe in our mission as leaders, we will do everything possible to assist all those working toward that mission to do it better. Offering clear, unvarnished feedback in performance management is a key aspect of the leader's role. Excellence is the goal, spurring both supervisors and employees well beyond mediocrity or undemanding adequacy.

WE AFFIRM AND RESPECT PEOPLE WHEN WE HOLD THEM TO HIGH STANDARDS AND THEN COMMUNICATE THAT WE BELIEVE THEY CAN MEET THOSE STANDARDS.

Informal Feedback

What are the ordinary means of providing feedback, managing workplace behavior, encouraging people to work efficiently and effectively toward goals, and achieving your mission? You begin with current and accurate job or position descriptions. Each person, whether employee or volunteer, needs to clearly understand his or her role, duties, and overall responsibilities. As previously discussed, you can't hire well without having a complete role description for the vacant position. Likewise, you can't supervise well without that same role description. Each person needs to understand how his or her role connects with the role descriptions of others on the staff and where the boundaries are between them. At the same time, flexibility should also be built into the job description. Job descriptions can change gradually or even precipitously as the needs of the organization change. The role of the pastor or supervisor is to monitor the change that is taking place. As a pastor, principal, or director, you provide immediate and informal feedback, often daily. You note the work, the problems, the small successes, the ongoing challenges, and the daily routine with specific, usually positive, and sometimes corrective communication. This can be a quick remark that you noticed the work being well done. I once worked with someone who was excellent at the quick note or e-mail acknowledging a small or large accomplishment or extending an offer to help if there was a problem. Practical and informal communication is not the same as micromanaging, which conveys a lack of confidence or trust in the staff member. The micromanager constantly tells people exactly how a job should be done with detailed instructions, with the effect that employees are discouraged and lose incentive.

As a leader, you should provide ordinary informal feedback often and consistently throughout the workweek and the work year. If there is an immediate work-related behavioral problem such as chronic tardiness, missed deadlines, problems with technology skills, issues with parishioner and client relationships, these problems should be handled as they arise. Don't wait for a formal review process to correct them. Meet with the staff member or volunteer quickly after the problem becomes evident and together work toward and agree on a solution for immediate implementation.

If you need to meet with a staff member to deal with a performance issue, do it privately. No one should be corrected in front of others. These meetings always begin with a presumption of respect and privacy. If you are angry, delay the meeting until you can be calm and rational.

In religious organizations, we are fortunate to have prayer as a resource in confronting difficult situations. We can ask God to guide our meeting and help us do and say the right thing. Prayer gives us context and perspective, so it helps to pray—for yourself and the employee—privately beforehand.

Formal Appraisal Process

Most organizations have policies requiring at least an annual review. As you strive to implement mission, the formal performance review process is key to assisting you in your role as pastor, principal, business manager, or director. There is movement in the secular world to have simpler but more frequent reviews. Most church organizations today strive toward consistently well-done annual reviews. As we learn to implement and value performance management, we can revise and improve our formal review procedures.

There are significant legal parameters surrounding the formal appraisal process. Because appraisals are used to determine salary increases, promotions, and even staff retention, the tool used must be implemented with training of supervisors and staff, needs to consistently measure the desired outcomes, and must be objective, fair, and nondiscriminatory. The measurements must be job related. Staff members have a right to know if they are meeting the expectations of the supervisor, and if not, what is required for improvement and what kinds of assistance they can expect toward achieving that improvement.

STAFF MEMBERS HAVE A RIGHT TO KNOW IF THEY ARE MEETING THE EXPECTATIONS OF THE SUPERVISOR, AND IF NOT, WHAT IS REQUIRED FOR IMPROVEMENT AND WHAT KINDS OF ASSISTANCE THEY CAN EXPECT TOWARD ACHIEVING THAT IMPROVEMENT.

Performance appraisal tools analyze a variety of criteria for judging a staff member's contributions to the organization. Some focus on the assessment of goals and objectives that have been prescribed and accomplished. Others focus on the knowledge and skills of the employee needed to succeed in the position.[2] Most tools also assess the personality and attitudinal traits necessary for success in the specific position and in the culture of the organization. A combination of these are often included in an assessment tool.

Employees have a right to know your expectations regarding the content and quality of their work. Therefore, staff members have a right to expect and experience a fair review process. While neither supervisors nor staffs look forward to performance reviews, you can make it a positive encounter for yourself and your employees. A positive review process is more likely when your staff members each have a clear understanding of your expectations. That begins with the carefully crafted and up-to-date job description discussed above, but a successful performance appraisal process also depends on the daily or ordinary supervisory process. Consistent informal communication mitigates surprises during the formal review process or especially the evaluation meeting. You have already called attention to the more significant difficulties as they happened or became apparent.

2. Max Messmer, *Human Resources Kit for Dummies*, 3rd ed. (Hoboken, NJ: John Wiley and Sons, 2012), 264–65.

Ordinarily, you begin the discussion with the person's positive qualities, as the performance review is a time to be specific about both positives and negatives. You can make the review process more meaningful and accurate if you work to make that process collaborative between you and the employee. Begin by having the staff member complete the evaluation tool independently and then return it to you. The employee's ability to be candid regarding his or her performance depends on several factors, beginning with the atmosphere of respect that is already part of your relationship. Have you had open, relevant, but informal discussions? Does the person know and understand your expectations? Does he or she feel confident they will be treated with respect even if there is need for a difficult conversation or confrontation on an issue or behavior? Is your employee comfortable discussing the positive aspects of his or her performance through the annual review period?

Many staff members can easily discuss their problems but are reticent to discuss their positive qualities. This may be a cultural, personal, or psychological obstacle. You make this easier by including as part of the tool a place to name concrete accomplishments, goals achieved, and job description responsibilities completed.

Likewise, the review tool asks the employee to name areas where goals have not been achieved or job responsibilities are not being met. The staff member will probably have a much better handle on achievements and problems than you will as the supervisor, depending on how closely you work with that person on a daily basis. For example, the pastor of a parish may be unaware of some of the director of religious education's specific accomplishments. The time of the review is an excellent opportunity for you to become aware of those achievements for each member of your team.

As the supervisor, you will also complete a draft of your version of the performance review tool. Leave yourself the chance to change your evaluation based on what you learn from the employee. There will be some positive achievements and issues that you see that your employee has not mentioned or does not recognize.

The review process becomes final with your version of the review, considering what your staff member has provided as input. Sometimes an employee won't agree with your final evaluation and might refuse to sign the completed performance appraisal. The signature means only that the staff member has received and read the review, not that he or she agrees with the evaluation. You never need to accede to a demand on the part of an employee to change an evaluation based on a disagreement. However, the employee can file a letter disputing the evaluation, and that letter should be placed in the personnel file along with your evaluation.

The most crucial part of the review process is the conversation between you and your staff member after each of you has completed the form. This conversation should be unhurried, private, and candid. I have seen supervisors who fill out the form and then hand it to the employee for signature with no conversation or input. Even if the appraisal is positive, this is very unsatisfying, and does little to promote the mission of the organization. Good, frank, appreciative conversation is both vital and productive. Begin the conversation by expressing your gratitude for what the person does and focus on that person's strengths and achievements. In most appraisals, this is the heart of the discussion and takes significant time.

The conversation must also include the problems, issues, and missed opportunities for that employee to have made positive contributions. Everyone has a right to know how they are doing in your eyes as their pastor or supervisor. Honesty is the highest priority. Be clear about what the person is doing well as well as those areas in which he or she is not meeting your expectations. For both pastoral and legal reasons, if your staff member is not meeting expectations, you cannot delay such observations until the moment of dismissal. Communicate problems respectfully and with nuance and understanding. Use specific examples whenever possible. Allow for silences.

There are legal implications if problems are not discussed. Staff members have a right to know of problem areas that might result in negative consequences. When an involuntary termination is a potential outcome, the leader will be asked to produce written documentation that the employee was told of the problems and given opportunities to correct them. When an involuntary termination is being considered, human resource professionals and legal counsel will immediately request copies of the formal review process as well as other documentation in consideration of the appropriateness of the termination.

PERFORMANCE APPRAISAL IS AN ESSENTIAL RESPONSIBILITY OF EVERY GOOD SUPERVISOR.

Everyone has a right to a performance appraisal. It is not just a policy requirement; it is an essential responsibility of every good supervisor. People need to share accountability for mission and so have a right to know how well they are doing in contributing to that mission. They also deserve the chance to know if they are not meeting your expectations, how to make corrections and improvements, and in what time frame. Sometimes they deserve or may request follow-up meetings. In such instances, prepare a plan that specifies how and when reevaluation will take place. If there are specific behavioral deficiencies, the performance appraisal tool should include a way to describe the corrected behaviors and how soon they will be reevaluated. This is called an "improvement plan" and is included in the file with the performance appraisal.

Performance Review Tools

What are the elements of a good performance appraisal tool? There are a wide variety of tools available through the National Association of Church Personnel Administrators (NACPA, www.nacpa.org), and the Society for Human Resources Management (shrm.org). There are tools that use primarily quantitative measures, others that focus on qualitative measures, and a third type commonly referred to as a "360-degree review." Quantitative reviews are ordinarily appropriate for jobs that have reported and verifiable quantitative goals, such as sales and customer service positions. Often, 360-degree reviews are used by boards in evaluating executive directors and are now regularly used in many dioceses and religious congregations to provide developmental feedback to ministerial staff and clergy. They incorporate feedback from clients, colleagues, staff, and leadership. You will find examples of these tools from the organizations we cited above as well as at the Leadership Roundtable (http://www.leadershiproundtable.org/tlr/aboutus/programs.html).

Choose a tool that is straightforward. You don't need a complex or highly numeric evaluative tool. A good tool includes a place to evaluate specific job responsibilities, an evaluation of workplace behaviors and characteristics that contribute to or detract from the accomplishment of mission, and a mutual establishment of goals and performance objectives for the next review period. As part of reviewing job responsibilities, you discuss revisions to the position description.

Common Errors

Drawn from one of the "resource bibles" for Human Resources in the corporate world,[3] here are some common mistakes during the appraisal process, applied to church organizations:

- Comparing employees to yourself and rating someone higher because he or she is like you.
- Comparing one employee to the others rather than to the standards required by the job description.
- Rating everyone highly. One priest said to us that he gave everyone in his department the highest possible rating because there wasn't enough money to pay market value for those positions. His view was that if we cannot recognize with money, then we recognize by superlative performance reviews. If everyone in an organization receives the highest rating, there is no way to distinguish between excellent and average performance. Likewise, when everyone receives a high rating, our standards may simply be too low. We fail to expect excellence from our staff members in implementing the mission.
- Holding unreasonably high standards. Supervisors who do this are incapable of recognizing outstanding or successful performance.
- The "halo effect": rating an employee highly because of one excellent part of their performance without objectively looking at the rest of their performance. The "halo effect," often a factor in hiring, may also muddy the performance appraisal process.
- Conversely, giving a negative overall rating because of one problematic part of the employee's performance.
- Rating more attractive and likable persons more favorably than others. It is great to be likeable, but the actual job performance must still be reviewed and considered carefully.

Conclusion

The formal performance appraisal process is a developmental rather than a disciplinary tool. Disciplinary actions normally happen during the ordinary work process. If there is a problem to be addressed, do so at the time the problem occurs. You may want to mention these problem situations during the performance appraisal, but corrective action should already be in place. For example, if you notice a repeated pattern of tardiness, address it when it happens. Do not wait until the performance appraisal. The formal review process is developmental, constructed to improve overall performance and effective mission implementation. If work-related problems have not yet been corrected adequately, you should include them in the improvement plan that is designed as part of the process. Reviews give you an opportunity to coach and mentor staff and to clarify your expectations. They give the pastoral leader a key opportunity to impact the accomplishment of the organization's mission, goals, and objectives.

3. Barbara Mitchel and Cornelia Gamlem, *The Big Book of HR, Revised and Updated Edition* (Wayne, NJ: Career Press, 2017), 187.

Components of an Effective Performance Management System

- An organizational culture that values performance excellence
- Individual assessment of staff and volunteers
- Tools that do not discriminate and are job related
- Review items consistent with strategic mission of the organization
- Usefulness as a developmental tool for groups and individuals
- Training of those who administer the tool as well as those who will be reviewed
- Effectiveness in assessing compensation and promotion

In chapter 7, we will examine compensation in the workplace, salary structure, payroll administration, and related legal issues.

7

Recognition and Compensation

Chapter Preview

In this chapter, Fr. Dave will:

- Acknowledge the key roles different forms of recognition play in the workplace.
- Understand the major elements of a compensation philosophy.
- Examine some of the legal parameters of compensation.
- Learn about salary structures and the basics of salary structure development.
- Discover the key components of efficient and consistent payroll administration.

Introduction

Staff members, both employees and volunteers, need recognition and rewards for their work and effectiveness. Recognition can include simple expressions of gratitude as well as formal and sometimes complicated financial reward systems. Everyone wants to be noticed and appreciated for their contributions in accomplishing the mission. Recognition provides a means for influencing outcomes and worker, volunteer, or minister engagement. This can begin with a specific targeted "thank you" from the manager to the employee, either publicly or privately, depending on the circumstances and the individual. Some people find public appreciation embarrassing and would rather have a private exchange. Recognition may also include letters of gratitude, celebrations and events, flowers, and gift cards. Employee recognition includes all the above, but naturally, also includes the financial rewards of fair compensation and benefits. This is often referred to as *total rewards*. It is important always to remember that volunteers do not receive financial rewards for their work, as this can cause legal issues for the organization. Giving financial rewards to volunteers may lead to allegations from the government that you are evading minimum wage requirements or failing to implement payment of payroll taxes and withholding requirements for those receiving compensation.

Compensation Philosophy

Even small church-based organizations, including parishes, have a compensation philosophy, even if it has never been made explicit or put in writing. A compensation philosophy includes the following:

- Legal consistency
- External equity
- Internal equity
- Merit pay decisions
- Administration
- Justice

There are many kinds of employee compensation. Base pay and bonuses are primary considerations in describing an organization's total rewards, but so are provisions for benefits, paid time off (PTO), work environment, and good management practices. We know that employees feel compensated when they are trusted, communicated with, included in planning for mission effectiveness, provided with job training, and considered for advancement, when they work in a pleasant workplace built around concepts of fairness and justice. Employees also value the potential for work-life balance as a nonfinancial type of compensation. These are also keys to staff retention. When people voluntarily leave a position, they often say they are leaving because they will make more money elsewhere. While this may be true, they may be leaving because some element of the workplace environment is stressful or even hostile. Often, people don't leave an organization, they leave a bad manager or an unhappy or stress-filled work environment.

Successful employers strive to make legal consistency and compliance with policies fundamental to their compensation philosophies and implementation. Most employers are compliant with the legal complexities of payroll and employee treatment. However, church organizations sometimes fail to pay enough attention to the legalities of compensation. We will discuss some of these legal issues later in this chapter.

Another element of a compensation philosophy is the organization's view of external equity. This is can be referred to as the philosophy of *lead, meet, or lag*.[1] Do the organization's compensation decisions lead the way in its marketplace? Organizations with the *lead* philosophy are convinced they get the best people by paying more than their competitors. The *meet* philosophy's employers compensate at the market rate, neither trying to lead nor fall behind their competitors. The *lag* philosophy says an employer can't afford to be a leader and can't even afford to be among those employers who "meet." Such employers know ahead of time they cannot pay the market rate but strive to build attractive missions and environments that offset differences in formal compensation. Many faith-based employers fall into this category.

Most employers claim they pay attention to questions of internal equity, that is, compensation fairness among current staff, but they sometimes make errors with unforeseen consequences. This may happen when, to attract a new hire, they offer a higher rate of pay than they are paying current employees. In faith-based communities, which are often behind the market rate in compensation, a situation can arise when, in order to fill a position, market rate must be paid even when internal equity is violated. For example, a parish might hire a business manager who makes more money than the pastoral associate or director of liturgy because market competition influences the compensation. Ministerial positions are more central to the mission and have higher experiential and academic requirements; they do not

1. Barbara Mitchel and Cornelia Gamlem, *The Big Book of HR*, rev. and updated ed. (Wayne, NJ: Career Press, 2017), 126.

exist in the general marketplace and are undervalued. Consequently, the parish might have to give raises to several people to avoid the conflict that will arise when the new hire's salary becomes known. One of the great workplace myths is that salary and wage information are confidential. Of course, it is *supposed* to be confidential, but it is amazing how much "confidential" information becomes common knowledge among staff.

Many employers have systems that include merit pay in compensation. Merit pay has many advantages in the management of an organization. It encourages accountability and enhanced individual and team performance. Merit pay requires that the organization make good judgments about individual performance by use of excellent assessment methods.[2] In small organizations, merit pay can be fraught with difficulty even though employers may use it to recognize exceptional work. If church employers want to implement a merit pay system, they should seek professional human resources advice. A simpler method of recognizing outstanding work is by using one-time bonuses. The advantage to this is that the bonus does not become part of the base pay, so it does not automatically recur the following fiscal year.

The administration of a payroll system must be transparent, tax compliant, legal, and easy enough to implement so that it is effective and provides all the support that an employer needs. All employees should understand the general administrative structure of the payroll system. When they understand the process and know where to take questions or address possible errors, they retain confidence in employers' intentions to administer compensation fairly and in a timely manner.

EMPLOYEE CONFIDENCE IN THE COMMITMENT OF AN ORGANIZATION OR PARISH TO A JUST WORKPLACE...BEGINS WITH THEIR TRUST IN THE COMPENSATION SYSTEM.

Promoting justice in the church workplace is at the foundation of this book. Justice in compensation is fundamental. Decision-making regarding compensation should be transparent and defensible. Employee confidence in the commitment of an organization or parish to a just workplace, let alone to justice in society, begins with their trust in the compensation system.

Legal Parameters

We previously discussed the importance of the Fair Labor Standards Act (FLSA) in employment law. Compensation is the focus of FLSA compliance, and compliance with its provisions is essential in compensation administration. Nonexempt employees are subject to the requirements of paid overtime as legislated by the FLSA. The normal workweek is defined by each place of employment and does not need to be the same as a calendar week. In other words, for some the normal workweek is from Monday through Sunday; for others, it may begin on Sunday or any other day of the week. Overtime pay is required for anyone who works more than forty hours in the defined workweek. Every hour beyond the forty hours is paid at time and a half or 150 percent of the hourly wage.

The daily schedule may be adjusted during the normal workweek so that, even if on a given day the nonexempt worker has worked more than eight hours, he or she may work fewer hours on other days of the work week so as not to exceed forty hours for the week. However, the schedule may not be adjusted beyond that workweek, even if the pay period is two weeks—that is, two weeks of work hours may not be averaged over two weeks. Each week must be considered and compensated separately, even when in

2. Shawn Smith and Rebecca Mazin, *The HR Answer Book: An Indispensable Guide for Managers and Human Resources Professionals*, 2nd ed. (New York: AMACOM, 2011), 111.

the same pay period. This is referred to as compensation time: the hours that are worked by nonexempt staff during the same workweek. Although faith-based organizations have not had a good record of properly compensating for overtime, compliance with FLSA has greatly improved.

Related to this discussion on required overtime pay for nonexempt employees, keep in mind that nonexempt staff persons may not "volunteer" to do their jobs. Nonexempt administrative assistants, for instance, may not volunteer to perform administrative assistant work as a contribution of time or talent to the organization or parish or project. This could be considered a way to pressure employees to accept less pay than they have earned. However, if an administrative assistant volunteered his or her time working in a way that has no relationship to their job description, such volunteer work could not be construed as a way of avoiding compensation responsibilities. If an administrative assistant volunteers his time to organize the food concession at the school carnival, this is not a part of the normal job description and would be appropriate. However, the assistant could not volunteer to organize and perform the administrative duties of the carnival because such work would resemble activities in his or her day-to-day job description.

A dilemma facing church employers is the issue of unauthorized overtime. Sometimes, employees work overtime, record the hours on their time sheets, and expect to be paid for the time worked. The employer must pay the employee for the time, but there are ways to remedy this. First, every employer needs a policy that requires preauthorization of overtime. The person working the overtime is obligated to get permission from his or her supervisor to work those extra hours. When the person works overtime without the required authorization, while the time worked must be paid, the worker may be disciplined for not getting permission. This discipline may be in the form of a verbal warning or written notice of policy violation. There will be times when a worker does not seek permission to work, but you as the supervisor agree with the decision to work even without permission. For example, a parish might have a maintenance worker who responds to an emergency, such as a boiler problem or a snowstorm, and works overtime hours without permission. This normally constitutes good independent decision-making and appropriate use of flexibility in policy implementation.

EVERY EMPLOYER NEEDS A POLICY THAT REQUIRES PREAUTHORIZATION OF OVERTIME.

Exempt employees who meet the duties test and salary basis test for exemption (see chapter 2) or those paid a salary may only have deductions from their salary on a full-day rather than an hourly basis. For example, sick days and vacation days are for full days and not calculated on hours or part of a day. An exempt employee who qualifies for a sick leave policy takes those days on a full-day basis. If exempt employees are present for half a day and then go home sick, they are not charged for a half sick day. Hours worked may be tracked but not for calculating compensation. They are often tracked for Affordable Care Act requirements, PTO benefits, implementation of the Family and Medical Leave Act (FMLA), and as a good management practice.

Unlike the legal parameters around compensation time for nonexempt employees, there is no such prohibition for exempt employees. However, caution should be exercised. Inherent in the definition of full-time exempt employees is the understanding that they work however many hours it takes to get the job completed. Therefore, there is no requirement for compensation time when exempt staff works more than forty hours in a work week. Compensation time may be granted if that time is not calculated on an hour-by-hour basis. Exempt staff should not be recording hours worked and then totaling those hours to request compensation time. If compensation time is given to exempt staff, it is usually granted only when full days of time have been worked in excess of the usual workweek. For example, a pastoral associate has worked one or two hours into the evening for several days. This is appropriate to the role of pastoral associate. If that same pastoral associate has worked a normal workweek and then is present for a parish retreat all day Saturday and Sunday, then it could be appropriate to give one or two days of compensation time for the two days of extra work that week. If granted, compensation time should be relatively close to the time when the extra time was worked. It should not be accumulated so that the organization is responsible for a week or two of extra PTO at the end of a fiscal year. Compensation time should not be considered compensable if the exempt staff member has not taken the time off by the time the position is terminated.

Salary Structures

Salary structures are compensation systems that have been developed by analyzing positions carefully and determining appropriate remuneration for each. The compensation philosophy is a key part in the development of these structures. The position analysis includes factors such as the academic background and competencies required to fill the position and the context and purpose of this position in the larger organization. These structures are often complex and are more often developed in large organizations rather than small ones. The results of these systems provide the organization with ranges for each position or for each group of positions. For example, there may be a range established for all secretaries in an organization though any individual secretary will be placed in that range differently dependent on experience, tenure, or competencies.

For smaller faith-based organizations, if there is a compensation system, it has probably been developed at a higher level of the organization. For example, many dioceses have developed compensation systems for teachers and principals in parochial schools. Dioceses may also have developed compensation ranges for many parish positions such as pastoral associates, directors of religious education, music ministers, and business managers. These ranges have been developed using position analysis information as well as salary survey information from parishes in the diocese. In most cases, these are suggested guidelines for compensation, and parishes may make exceptions. When ranges are updated every two or three years, new calculations offer helpful information to those making compensation decisions in parishes. In some dioceses, the compensation levels for teachers and perhaps principals are mandated.

Salary ranges may also be developed for small organizations without the complexity of a formal salary structure-analysis process. They are usually developed for positions by reviewing salaries for current employees and comparing salary survey information from the diocese or comparable organizations. Salary range development offers many advantages. Because many small employers find merit pay difficult to implement, they have consistently used annual percentage increases or cost-of-living increases. One consequence, however, can be that long-term employees eventually earn more than their positions warrant. For example, a school secretary may have been given percentage increases consistently until that person now earns more than some teachers. With salary ranges, the employer determines the top of the range as well as the low end of the range. The top of the range indicates that position's highest level of worth to the organization, so that when an employee reaches the top of the range, the automatic increases stop until the salary range is adjusted. Ranges are ordinarily reviewed and adjusted every two to three years.

When salary ranges are first implemented, there may be outliers at the bottom and the top of the ranges. Once the ranges have been determined, you may find that you have one or two people who are being paid below the range for the position. You may give increases beyond normal increases at one time or for a couple of years until those salaries reach the appropriate range. Likewise, immediately following the implementation of salary ranges, you may find that there are a few people above the appropriate range. After looking at the position analysis, you may decide to decrease the salaries to the meet the requirements of the range system. You may communicate, preferably in person, the rationale with a staff member that his or her position does not meet the criteria for the salary being paid. However, because this decision is likely to create conflict, it might simply be impractical, especially if you do not want to lose the person who holds the position. In that case, you may stop providing increases until the salary reaches the appropriate range.

Salary ranges are particularly helpful in determining starting salaries for open positions. Most employers start people below the first quartile of the designated range. If the new hire has a lot of experience in a similar position, and in other ways is an excellent person for the job, you may start the person in the first half of the range. If, however, you start someone higher than the midpoint of the range, you risk alienating current staff members who started lower or who are not earning as much currently. You also face the likelihood that your new hire will reach the top of the range too quickly and thereby have his or her pay frozen for at least a year or two.

Payroll Administration

Small employers have a history of doing payroll in their own offices, but as payroll has become more complex, most have turned to payroll providers. Payroll has major legal and financial implications, so it is vital to do it properly. Competent payroll administrators should demonstrate the flexibility and knowledge required to provide services to religious employers with their special needs. For example, clergy have the option to not have taxes withheld. Most clergy do even though they are not legally required to do so. If they do not have taxes withheld, they must file quarterly returns with estimated taxes paid. Vowed men and women religious do not pay taxes at all if they are members of a religious congregation that is recognized as such by the *Official U.S. Catholic Directory*. Most payroll providers do not understand this exception in the tax code, and, therefore, have no protocols in their systems for this exception.

Using a payroll provider or administrator ensures that your payroll is being administered by someone who stays current with changing rules and intricacies of federal, state, and local tax structures. Payroll administrators may also provide many other human resources systems to supplement the systems in place at the local level. They can provide time and attendance records, benefits administration services, and basic employee data information. In the case of Catholic parishes, it is becoming the norm for the diocese to provide a single payroll provider, allowing each parish to make input to the system with payroll funds drawn from the local parish or school bank account. Such standardized payroll systems apply a uniform chart of accounts and provide the same benefits deductions across the diocese. Some dioceses have moved to a completely centralized payroll system with everyone paid from the diocese, with each parish and school reimbursing the diocese for these costs. When standardized and centralized payroll systems are used, there can be significant cost savings because fee negotiations for these services are based on a much larger number of employees and employers being served.

Payroll checks must always be issued on time and without caveats such as requests not to cash a paycheck until the following Monday, after the Sunday collection is deposited. Payroll is a legal contract that employers must honor to the minutest detail.

Recordkeeping is also a vital part of payroll administration. Time sheets or time records, especially for nonexempt employees are critical. Time sheets must be signed by the employee and the supervisor and held for at least three years. In today's electronic world, these may be set up with electronic recordkeeping and electronic signatures, but retention of these records is still required. Should records get lost or if they were never retained, a nonexempt employee could file charges with your state's Department of Labor claiming he or she was not paid overtime for any period going back three years. The employee will likely win the case, requiring the employer to forfeit the back pay, usually with punitive charges added. Employers can successfully defend themselves from such charges by simply presenting the employee's signed time sheets and payroll records demonstrating he or she received the wages owed. The burden of proof is on the employer.

Conclusion

Employers must include compensation decisions and administration among their most essential responsibilities. When systematized well, the implementation will seem invisible to both leadership and employees. Without compensation structures in place, employers get bogged down with complicated implementations of compensation decisions and preoccupied with time-consuming administrative issues. Paying attention to details at the beginning of compensation implementation yields smooth administration unburdened by constant intervention and problem solving.

In chapter 8, we will review issues surrounding employee benefits.

8

Employee Benefits

Chapter Preview

In this chapter, Fr. Dave will:

- Examine the concept of total compensation.
- Learn some of the legal parameters around employee benefits.
- Understand and examine the lists of the following:
  - ♦ Legally mandated benefits;
  - ♦ Voluntary benefits.
- Study benefits eligibility, recordkeeping, and benefits communication.

Introduction

When candidates apply for a position in an organization, they inquire about compensation but are slower to ask about benefits. Yet the importance of benefits to an employee is significant. Some years ago, as we sought ways to improve our employee benefits package in the Catholic Archdiocese of Chicago, we conducted a random employee survey. We learned that employees would have preferred receiving better direct pay than we offered, but as they also communicated clearly, they understood the realities. If our benefits had not been comparable to what they might receive in other organizations, they would not have been able to stay with us. Mediocre benefits would more likely lead to low retention rates more so than poor compensation. Employee benefits provide a safety net for employees and their families. Even in small faith-based employers with attractive and important missions, most employees are unwilling to sacrifice good benefits.

We also know that candidates and employees undervalue the financial worth of their benefits when evaluating their compensation. Candidates might ask what benefits are provided but fail to ask the level of employee contribution required or the rules for eligibility. Instead, they tend to focus on base pay. Most employers recognize the importance of benefits in job satisfaction, work performance, mission effectiveness, and staff retention. However, most also recognize they have not always communicated the importance and value of benefits to their employees.

Some Legal Parameters

The array of legal parameters around employee benefits is too complex and extensive to adequately cover here. However, we will briefly describe significant legalities as they apply to parishes, schools, and other church-based employers. Many of the legal complexities are handled at the level of the benefits providers and the larger entity from which the benefits are initiated. For example, in Catholic parishes, schools, and agencies, legal compliance issues of provided benefits are usually managed at the diocesan level. This is even true in those dioceses that have separately incorporated parishes but where benefits are still handled by the diocesan human resources offices. Likewise, pension administrators, insurance companies, and other benefits providers work diligently to ensure legal compliance for the benefits they provide.

Legally Mandated Benefits

The most important mandated benefit is *Social Security*. All lay employees are required to participate in Social Security and, therefore, pay the employee portion of Social Security taxes. The employee portion of Social Security is a percentage of income with an annual maximum on which these taxes are paid. The annual maximum salary changes each year. The employer is also required to match the employee portion of Social Security taxes. These taxes are commonly referred to as FICA (Federal Insurance Compensation Act) payments. Clergy relate to Social Security under the self-employed rubric, and most dioceses require their clergy to participate in Social Security, though it was not required of clergy in the original Social Security legislation. Withholding of Social Security taxes for clergy has some technical considerations. For questions regarding these processes, you should consult your office for clergy, your chief financial officer, or the diocesan human resources office.

Medicare provides hospital and medical benefits to people sixty-five and older. It is financed by payroll taxes on all employees and employers. Withholding taxes for Medicare is mandatory, is a percentage of income, and, unlike Social Security, there is no annual ceiling. When a benefits-eligible employee reaches age sixty-five, the employer may not require the individual to move from the employee health plan to Medicare. If the employee has enrolled in Medicare Part A, the employee health plan is primary and Medicare is considered secondary. Medicare Part A does not have a premium attached so employees should be encouraged to enroll in Part A when they become eligible at their sixty-fifth birthday. Medicare Part A covers inpatient care or a skilled nursing facility. Part B is for doctors and other medical services. Ordinarily, employees who remain on the employer plan would not enroll in Part B until they are no longer eligible for an employer-sponsored health plan, such as at retirement. Medicare Part B has a significant monthly premium.

The *Family and Medical Leave Act of 1993* (FMLA) provides for employee leave in situations that include the birth or adoption of a child, or to care for themselves or an immediate family member with a serious illness. This is unpaid leave, but the employer continues providing employee benefits during the leave. The employer may require the employee to use any accrued paid time off, such as sick leave or vacation days, as part of the leave. The employer also guarantees the person's job or a comparable position on return from leave. Small employers may not be required to participate in FMLA if they have fewer than fifty employees. However, these eligibility rules can be complicated in dioceses. A parish might have fewer than fifty employees, but the number of employees in the diocese far exceeds the minimum of fifty. In many dioceses, especially those structured as a single legal entity known as Corporation Sole, which includes all parishes, schools, and agencies, the diocese is considered the legal employer and, therefore, FMLA is mandated. FMLA can be difficult to manage because there are complexities to be considered such as its interaction with the Americans with Disabilities Act, employee eligibility, and leave structures. Access to a human resources professional is very helpful when implementing FMLA as well as other employee benefits.

Unemployment Insurance is a temporary and partial income replacement program for those who have become unemployed through no fault of their own. It is managed and administered by each state and, therefore, rules vary, based on each state's policies. There are different ways in which states receive reimbursement from employers for the costs of unemployment insurance. Because of their tax-exempt status, church employers are usually exempt from unemployment mandates, but many faith-based employers and dioceses have chosen to participate because unemployment insurance serves as a safety net for terminated employees.

Another important safety net program, *Worker's Compensation,* is a benefit provided to an employee who is injured in a work-related incident or contracts a work-related illness. In most places, worker's compensation regulations derive from the state and are covered by the employer's property and liability insurance program.

Additional Legal Considerations

While there are numerous additional legal issues dealing with employee benefits, the only ones we will highlight are those with basic and universal application. The first of these is the *Health Insurance Portability and Accountability Act* (HIPPA). It provides for continuity in group health coverage, and it addresses important considerations regarding health information privacy protection. Health insurance portability is a major concern for employees when moving from one position to another. The HIPPA act protects their right to receive coverage from their next employer without fear of limitations based on preexisting conditions. HIPPA also requires well-known protections for employee health privacy. It mandates that insurance companies, medical providers, and employers protect the privacy of each employee's medical information. Employee files with medical information such as disability requests, sick leave, and FMLA activity, and any other kind of health information must be housed in locked files accessible only to those individuals with a significant right to such information such as the employee's supervisor. In faith-based organizations, we have sometimes found ourselves in violation of HIPPA with very good intentions, but in violation, nonetheless. In the Archdiocese of Chicago's Pastoral Center, we once routinely posted prayer requests for persons who were sick, injured, or facing surgery. With HIPPA, we still post requests for prayer but only with the employee's permission, and we provide only as much information as the employee is willing to share. Employees appreciate the prayer support but often want limited information regarding their illness shared.

Political realities influence governmental healthcare laws, and at this writing, the status of the *Affordable Care Act* (ACA)—sometimes referred to as "Obamacare"—is in flux, and the possible changes to this act or even its repeal remain in question. If it is repealed, we do not know the implications for the future role of the federal government in providing health insurance for at least some citizens. Faith-based employers are affected by whatever changes may occur. Our organizations have had many issues and questions regarding the implementation of the ACA, yet most faith-based organizations remain supportive of the large numbers of people who have health insurance who could not obtain it before the plan's implementation. Catholic social teaching regards basic healthcare as a human right. Administration of the ACA has created new requirements on employer-based health plans and their payroll and benefits administrators. For church employers, the next steps in the revision or replacement of the ACA are of vital importance. Do keep yourself aware of developments and expect guidance from diocesan support services.

Voluntary Benefits

Except for the mandated benefits just discussed, employers are not required to provide employee benefits, but do so for the sake of attracting and retaining the best people to accomplish the mission. For the most part, without good benefits, good people won't join us or stay with faith-based organizations.

Health and Welfare Benefits

The first category of benefits we will identify are those usually referred to as health and welfare benefits. The following list is not exhaustive but includes the most often provided benefits in this category. They include the following:

- *Health insurance*: This is the most commonly provided benefit in this category and the most expensive to both the employer and the employee. There are many types of health coverage, including:
    - ♦ Traditional fee-for-service (indemnity)
    - ♦ Preferred provider organizations (PPO)
    - ♦ Health maintenance organizations (HMO)
    - ♦ Point-of-service plans (POS)
    - ♦ High-deductible plans
- *Dental plans*
- *Vision care*
- *Prescription plans*: For most employers, prescription coverage is embedded in the health insurance program, but for other employers, it may be provided separately.
- *Wellness programs* encourage employees to engage in healthy lifestyles to keep healthcare costs down. The savings may be shared with employees in the forms of incentives, gifts, or discounts on premiums.
- *Health-savings accounts* (HSAs) are usually part of high-deductible plans that establish special savings accounts and provide tax saving advantages.
- *Long-term care insurance* is sometimes offered as a voluntary benefit and provides financial supplements when a person is in a nursing home, assisted living, home healthcare, hospice care, and so on.
- *Employee assistance programs* (EAPs) provide employees assistance in times of difficulty for themselves or family members. In faith-based organizations, this is sometimes one of the services an organization itself may provide. For example, in many Catholic dioceses, Catholic Charities or Catholic Social Services may provide the EAP along with appropriate confidentiality measures.

Retirement Plans

Retirement plans are basic to the long-term well-being and security of employees. Effective plans are one part of a three-part approach to a successful retirement. Retirement programs recognize the role of government programs, Social Security and Medicare, individual planning and savings, and retirement income provided through qualified pension vehicles. Employers are moving away from traditional pension plans called defined benefit plans because they are difficult to keep properly funded. Funding requirements fluctuate each year with changing market returns and interest rates. Defined contribution plans, also known as 401(k) plans and in the nonprofit world, 403(b) plans, are more commonly used to provide funds from both the employer and the employee to grow savings for retirement. These plans feature the advantage of managing predictable funding requirements. They are portable, flexible, and ordinarily provide opportunities for employees to make additional tax-exempt contributions to the plan subject to annual limitations in the federal tax code.

Paid Time Off

Paid time off benefits include the following, but again this list is not exhaustive:

- *Vacation days*: Vacation time should not be cumulative beyond about fifteen to eighteen months. In other words, vacation days may only be accrued to a maximum number for a year to perhaps eighteen months. Allowing for accrual of vacation days beyond these limits sets up the organization to owe the employee for unused vacation time of several weeks to months. Since in most states, vacation days are compensable at termination, the employer could face a significant bill for unused vacation time.
- *Paid holidays*: The number of paid holidays per year is ordinarily set by policy, but the calendar for these days is likely to vary from one year to the next.
- *Sick leave* or annual sick-day allowance is usually cumulative up to a maximum number of days. The maximum is also identified in the personnel policies.
- *Personal days*: One to three days per year are usually provided for personal business.
- *Leaves of absence* such as bereavement leaves or personal leaves.
- *Retreat time* is especially appropriate in church organizations for ministerial staff, vowed religious, and clergy.
- *Professional development* time and funds may be granted in some organizations, such as a week to attend a conference related to one's work or ministry.
- *Paid time off* (PTO): Some employers have moved to PTO plans that combine sick leave, personal days, and vacation days. In other words, a certain number of days per year are provided for time away from the job regardless of the reason. These days may be used for sick leave, vacation days, personal days, and so on. A disadvantage for this type of plan becomes evident when employees come to work sick, protecting days available for vacation. During flu season, sick employees who come to work may very well be creating more sick employees, which is, of course, unhealthy for both the organization and its clients.

Income Replacement Plans

- *Life insurance*: Many employers provide term life insurance for employees that may provide options for employees to purchase additional coverage and take advantage of more favorable group rates.

- *Short-term disability insurance* is sometimes offered by employers when they do not have sick-leave policies. It may also be offered as an employee-paid benefit that can be helpful to an employee before he or she has accumulated significant sick-leave days.
- *Long-term disability insurance* provides a percentage of annual income replacement usually until age sixty-five for disabled employees who become no longer able to work or the employee is eligible for retirement and social security benefits.

Conclusion

Employee benefits eligibility is established by policy and by contract with benefits providers. For example, premiums set by health insurance providers are partially determined by the eligibility requirements of the organization. If the employer establishes a thirty-hour workweek for eligibility for health insurance, the provider knows that the base population being covered is healthy enough to work thirty hours and is a better risk.

The importance of good recordkeeping in benefits administration can't be overemphasized. Employers need to keep track of attendance, employee payments, and payroll deductions for benefits, use of tax-deferred means of paying those costs by the employee, enrollment dates, family information, and many other pieces of data.

Employee benefits are expensive but well worth providing. Employees sometimes undervalue their benefits. They often don't understand the costs to the employer and may fail to recognize the security their benefits provide them and their families. For small employers, including faith-based organizations, clear communication about benefits remains a significant area for improvement. Effective benefits communication explains benefits thoroughly, delineates options and choices for employees, and clearly outlines the costs that will be charged for each benefit to the employee. Many employers issue an *annual total compensation statement* that individualizes reports to each employee, including base pay, bonus pay, payroll taxes paid by the employer, and the cost to the employer of each benefit that has been provided or offered and accepted. Employees are often surprised at the amount of money being spent in addition to direct pay. This knowledge is valuable to the employee and the employer. Many excellent online communications options have become available to assist employers for reporting online information to staff on demand rather than only through an annual printed document.

In chapter 9, we will discuss succession planning, personnel transitions, and termination.

9

Personnel Transitions and Termination

Chapter Preview

In this chapter, Fr. Dave will:

- Learn about succession planning as a prelude to terminations.
- Examine voluntary terminations.
- Study the critical and difficult topic of just involuntary terminations.

Introduction

Change is inevitable and unremitting. Change is also difficult. We often underestimate its effects on us individually and on our organizations. Seldom are these dynamics more apparent than during times of personnel transitions, particularly terminations. So, it is that the time we invest in hiring well mitigates time spent dealing with difficult personnel situations or difficult staff members who do not live up to their original promises of competence and collaboration. Often, staff changes come about through normal changes in the lives of employees and volunteers who decide to leave our organizations. Sometimes, however, disappointing performance or behavior prompts such changes, and we, as leaders, must deal with those situations.

Succession Planning

At times of personnel transition or staffing change, employers can make good use of a valuable strategic tool, succession planning. It is the process "used by organizations to identify and prepare employees who have the potential skills and abilities to move into key positions when the incumbent leaves the job."[1] In succession planning, you identify people with the knowledge and competencies to fill key positions before vacancies occur. In small organizations, you may think you don't have the staffing depth to identify persons within the organization. However, if you have identified the abilities needed to

1. Barbara Mitchel and Cornelia Gamlem, *The Big Book of HR*, rev. and updated ed. (Wayne, NJ: Career Press, 2017), 22.

fill a position, you have already accomplished the first phase of succession planning. Many vacancies can be foreseen. Others result from sudden terminations or even a death. If possible, you identify a person who could be moved into a mission-critical vacant position. Recognizing potential successors for key leadership positions protects the mission and ministry of the organization and lets staff, clients, and parishioners know you will continue to serve effectively. Succession planning is a key factor in comprehensive strategic planning.

Voluntary Terminations

Voluntary terminations are those initiated by an employee. They include resignations and retirements. It is preferable to ask the employee to put the resignation in writing, including the reason for the termination, such as a new job, seeking higher compensation, retirement, relocation, and so on. The resignation letter should include an effective date. As an employer, you may ask for a minimum amount of notice to be given, but you may not require it.

Occasionally, an employee may get angry, resign abruptly, and leave the office. This is a legally binding resignation. A written resignation is not required in this situation. An oral resignation should be followed up with a registered letter to the employee accepting the resignation and providing the person with information regarding return to the workplace to retrieve personal items, outlining available benefits if any, and providing a date for a final pay check. If the angry employee, who has verbally resigned, returns with an apology and wants to rescind his or her resignation, be very cautious about accepting that request. This employee has already indicated that he or she is angry or unhappy in their job, and one way he or she handles difficulties is by quitting. Such a resignation *may* be an opportunity to deal with a difficult situation without the likelihood of legal difficulties, such as a charge of unfair termination, and without providing unemployment compensation because it is a voluntary resignation.

Retirements are usually not a surprise. People frequently talk about upcoming plans for retirement openly and with great anticipation. This presents the opportunity for succession planning to be implemented, especially if the person retiring holds a key position in the parish or organization. At the very least, the search process for a replacement can be initiated when the individual officially announces his or her plans. It is very important that supervisory or leadership people in the organization never introduce a conversation about retirement. Asking a person about retirement before he or she has initiated such a discussion can result in a charge of age discrimination. After the person has brought up the topic, leadership can be very encouraging and supportive. Retirements mean additional conversations regarding benefits and initiation of a retirement plan. The retiree should be referred to the people in the organization or the diocesan human resources office who can explain the process and provide the critical information.

ASKING A PERSON ABOUT RETIREMENT BEFORE HE OR SHE HAS INITIATED SUCH A DISCUSSION CAN RESULT IN A CHARGE OF AGE DISCRIMINATION.

Exit interviews are very helpful to employers. These interviews invite the person leaving the organization to answer some questions about the workplace that might be useful in evaluating its culture, management, and retention strategies. Questions may include the following:

- What did you like best about your job?
- What did you like least about your job?

- Do you have suggestions for improving workflow processes and management?
- Did you receive appropriate support and feedback in the performance of your job responsibilities?
- Would you encourage others to work here?
- Was there anything specific about your work experience here that contributed to your decision to move to a position outside of this organization?
- What else would help us that we have not asked about?

All who resign, whether orally or in writing, should receive a letter accepting the resignation and providing information they will need to make this transition successfully. This letter should include final paycheck information, any available benefits with their ending dates, computer security protocols, return of organization-owned equipment and identification badges, and scheduled date for the exit interview. Naturally, a letter accepting a resignation should include gratitude for the service and engagement of this employee in the mission and ministry of the faith-based community he or she has served.

Involuntary Terminations

Involuntary terminations—those initiated by the employer—are far more difficult and complicated. They are fraught with legal complications and are among the most challenging responsibilities for anyone in management or leadership. There are several types of involuntary terminations. Reductions-in-force are necessary at times, usually for financial reasons. This is sometimes referred to as a layoff, but for most church employers, the term *layoff* fails to accurately describe the situation. *Layoff* is used when there is some possibility of calling people back into the same workplace when finances or the situation changes. You often hear the term in manufacturing companies when they "lay off" personnel while retooling a factory or preparing for a new product, unsure of its success or required production.

In churches, schools, or other types of nonprofit venues, reductions usually happen when revenue does not match expenses and action must be taken to keep the organization viable and financially stable. The selection of staff for the reduction is difficult, and the rationale must be defensible and objective. If the rationale for reduction is not carefully designed, the implementation of a reduction-in-force may be considered discriminatory. For example, in a school where older teachers are more highly compensated than younger teachers, it can be tempting to terminate the most experienced because you may need to let go fewer to achieve the same financial results. However, age discrimination will be the first thing an antidiscrimination adjudicatory body, such as the Equal Employment Opportunity Commission (EEOC) will analyze. The EEOC will ask whether an ethnic or age group was disproportionally affected by the choices made in terminations for financial reasons.

Some selection criteria will simply decree that those who were hired most recently will be the first to be terminated. However, the mission of the organization or school could be jeopardized if you use that rationale. Perhaps the school leadership decided that, to be relevant to today's parents and children, technology must be an essential part of the curriculum, but the most recently hired person is the only technology instructor. The rationale "last hired, first fired" would jeopardize the school's financial viability, the very reason for reduction. The rationale for a reduction-in-force must be clearly thought out, objective, nondiscriminatory, put in writing, and distributed to those affected.

Reductions-in-force may only affect one person in a small organization. For example, it may be necessary to reduce the size of a parish staff by one person to achieve a balanced budget. The decision must also be based on a rationale that considers staffing priorities and the strategic plans of the parish. Care must be taken that the decision can be justified for real reasons related to mission and finances.

Another type of involuntary termination happens during a reorganization of staff. The parish or organization decides to go in a new direction or meet previously unmet needs by altering the composition of the staff. These can be valid and important decisions, though not easy ones. Perhaps the parish has decided that, while it has two support staff members, neither speaks Spanish, now increasingly needed in the parish. One of those support staff members may have to be replaced by a Spanish-speaking staff member.

Sometimes, church employers are tempted to call a termination a "reorganization" when the termination is for another reason. It may feel more pastoral to tell a poorly performing employee that his or her position is being eliminated rather than to confront him or her with the truth of their poor performance. However, that lack of candor will be unmasked quickly once a new person is hired and the former employee files a charge of wrongful termination. To avoid a charge of falsely identifying a *termination* as a *reorganization*, you must be scrupulously honest that the position is being eliminated for strategic mission reasons and not as a ruse for avoiding a different kind of involuntary termination.

The most common type of involuntary termination is for poor performance, poor workplace habits, lack of ability to collaborate successfully with other staff members, or unethical conduct. Sometimes this is called "termination for cause" but all the involuntary terminations we discuss in this chapter are "just cause" terminations as opposed to "at-will" terminations (see chapter 2). None of these decisions is capricious or without consideration for the employee and the employer.

Just termination processes for performance and behavior require established policies that specify clear expectations of every employee, including those regarding performance. Polices must be communicated to reflect an ethical culture and standards basic to the core of the organization and its leadership.

Progressive discipline is the tool used to be sure a problem employee has been informed about the problem and been given a chance to correct it. Progressive discipline is the use of oral and written warnings, perhaps followed by other actions such as suspension with or without pay, stating the problems and how they can be corrected within a specific time frame to demonstrate improvement. As disciplinary warnings progress, they normally warn that failure to improve may result in termination. Some organizations have precise and detailed protocols, but that can be challenging and paralyze an employer with rigid procedural details. The progressive discipline protocols in union contracts are often detailed and precisely codified, making compliance with them difficult. However, compliance is possible when the supervisor pays attention to the details and patiently follows the designated steps in the progressive discipline process.

Most employers have policies that define progressive discipline processes to address issues as they arise. However, implementations of progressive discipline protocols depend on the nature of the problem. There are some issues that do not warrant progressive discipline, and they must be dealt with immediately and decisions made quickly. Such instances include theft from staff members or the organization, material misrepresentation on application documents or other employee materials, threatening or violent behavior, and selling or using illegal drugs on the job. Because no list can exhaust the possibilities of egregious offenses for which you may bypass progressive discipline, your policies should state that the organization reserves the right to make such decisions considering one of these offenses.

Faith-based employers often have difficulty holding staff accountable for satisfactory performances, let alone excellence. At the same time, church leaders often struggle to define expectations and aspirations clearly, while providing training, coaching, and management that makes excellence possible. Sometimes church leaders think that maintaining high expectations conflicts with being pastoral. In fact, the opposite is true. It is pastoral to tell people the truth, and it is pastoral to believe in your mission. It is pastoral to lead with dignity and promote the dignity of each person on the staff. What is *not* pastoral is making demands disrespectfully or so subtlety and indirectly that people do not know what is expected of them. All this connects to the leadership services of performance management and appraisals (see chapter 6). The difficult conversations confronting problem behaviors or lack of good job performance are necessary responsibilities for any designated leader.

SOMETIMES CHURCH LEADERS THINK THAT HOLDING HIGH EXPECTATIONS CONFLICTS WITH BEING PASTORAL. IN FACT, THE OPPOSITE IS TRUE.

It is never easy to terminate a problem employee. The church leader or supervisor must act with confidence when faced with the prospect of implementing an involuntary termination, especially one related to performance or behavior. Church leaders sometimes question themselves when these actions are necessary. Such questioning is good. Even when the reasons for the termination are justified and will resolve a problem, the action is still difficult to implement. Personal assurance of a just and moral termination decision rises from the decision-maker's knowledge that he or she

1. was clear with the employee about difficulties;
2. confronted, in most situations, the behaviors or performances more than once;
3. gave the employee time and resources to correct the problem.

When these steps have been taken, the church employer can feel confident that the decision, though difficult, is both pastoral and just. The leader can feel relieved that a challenging problem has been resolved. Meanwhile, pastoral leaders respect that, at least for the short term, a person's life has been significantly changed, and this can never be taken lightly.

Consulting a human resources professional or an employment attorney is an important step before implementing an involuntary termination for performance reasons. These professionals will always ask to see the file with the documentation leading to the decision. It is not their role to question your management decision about the suitability of the employee, though occasionally this is appropriate; rather, they are looking to see if you are ready to implement the decision. Often, the professional will understand the difficulty but advise that you are not ready to terminate the employee without risking serious consequences for the organization. The documentation may be insufficient or dated, or too little time may have been granted to the employee to fix the problem. For the manager or supervisor, slowing down the process can be difficult but will pay off in the long run. Emotions can run high in these situations and a cooling-off period can be very effective. The last thing you want, as the leader, is for a termination to end up in a lawsuit or complaint with the Department of Labor. The human resources professional or the labor attorney will protect both the employee and the organization and should be engaged in these difficult situations.

The involuntary termination meeting, whether for financial, reorganization, or performance reasons, is best scheduled toward the end of the day early in the week. The meeting should be short and direct. There should be no small talk before breaking the news to the employee who is being terminated. Someone else should be present for the meeting, such as the parish business manager, a representative from the diocesan human resources office, or associate pastor. The reasons for the termination should be provided verbally and briefly. Two or three sentences summarizing the ongoing difficulties are enough. The termination meeting is not the time to debate merits of the decision. A letter should be given to the employee stating the requirements for return of organization property, an outline of severance benefits, and the potential costs to the employee for those benefits. For example, the employee may be eligible for extended healthcare coverage through the employer's plan, but the employee will probably pay the premium for that coverage.

Ordinarily, when people are terminated, they leave the workplace that day and take their personal belongings with them. This is easier when the workday is ending, but this is not an inflexible rule. Sometimes being escorted from the workplace has serious morale effects on both those being dismissed and on those who are retained. It is often better to have this take place toward the beginning of the week, so the rest of the staff can be told that the person has left and so that they can be reassured of their own role, possible change in responsibilities, and standing in the organization.

There are times when the terminated employee will ask for the opportunity to resign rather than be terminated. There is usually no problem with granting this request, but the facts of the termination must remain in the file along with the request. The documentation must reflect the truth. Ordinarily, a resignation in this situation will not result in the inability of the person to collect unemployment. That happens only if the performance issues are related to egregious misconduct.

What benefits are sometimes provided to terminating employees? These may vary depending on the reason for the termination. For example, if people are leaving because of finances or reorganization, you may want to offer outplacement services or extended healthcare benefits at no or low cost. Sometimes it is appropriate to offer a severance package that consists of financial benefits or related supplements that extend beyond routine policy-driven benefits provided to departing employees. When you offer severance benefits, you may also ask the employee to sign a release from potential legal charges related to the termination. If you decide to ask for a release, you need to involve an employment attorney in the writing of this document.

Conclusion

One of the goals of this book has been to demonstrate that faith-based organizations can implement professional and effective human resources practices while retaining their identities as church employers. Transitions and terminations put this premise to the test, but it is a test we can pass with flying colors. In church workplaces, we have the gift and the strength of a strong ethical system founded on faith-based values and traditions. In the face of difficult personnel decisions, we know those decisions must be based on justice to the individual as well as justice to the organization and the mission. For the most part, we operate on funds donated to us by mission stakeholders, ordinary people donating from their strong sense of stewardship. We are responsible to those people for inspiring and even demanding excellence in each of us who collaborate in the mission.

10

Frequently Asked Questions

In the introduction to this book, Fr. Dave is the new pastor of St. Michael's, a parish with a school. He, like so many first-time pastors, immediately realizes he has had wonderful education and formation for priesthood, but little training in management of a small and vitally important organization. In this book, I have attempted to address the concerns of designated leaders of many types of faith-based organizations, but the image of Fr. Dave as the prototype of so many pastors with whom I have been fortunate enough to work is in the background of everything discussed.

All church management concerns are present to Fr. Dave as he begins his new assignment. However, my experience has included many opportunities to work with seminarians, newly ordained clergy, and pastors in their first assignment. I have loved the opportunity to work with people and teach some of the basics of human resources infrastructure to them, but pastors in their first assignment are the leaders who are most likely to have a firsthand experience of the complications of working with staff and volunteers. Their interest in human resources is not academic or hypothetical. Sometimes people management issues become evident before they've even begun that first assignment. With this experience in mind, I take this opportunity to address a few of the immediate questions that new pastors face during their first days into their first years as pastor, keeping in mind that true expertise in people leadership is a lifelong endeavor.

1. Are there effective ways to handle the transition into a new pastorate? What is the change process like?

Change is always difficult and requires attention, patience, prayer, and dialogue with friends, mentors, and spiritual directors. The change process evokes a variety of emotions in all the people affected by the change, including the new pastor, the pastor who is leaving the parish, staff, parish leadership, and parishioners. There is a series of small books that I highly recommend assisting with this process, called *Navigating Pastoral Transitions*. These books are listed in the bibliography and include very practical tools for pastors, parish staffs, and parish leadership.

A colleague and friend, Fr. Robert Heidenreich, a very successful long-time pastor in the Archdiocese of Chicago, describes the first several months of the new pastor's term as the honeymoon phase. It is a temporary period of trust and respect as the new pastor and the parishioners get to know one another. It is a wonderful time to build a more permanent foundation of trust that will facilitate inevitable change and dealing with difficulties. The new pastor can build mutual trust and respect during this phase by his behavior and actions. He works to be a good listener, is present and available to people, strives to remember names, collaborates with and learns about staff and parish organizations, and provides excellent pastoral ministry such as hospital visits, school presence, good liturgical presence, and attention to homilies.

One of the tools that some new pastors have used is to write a letter to his new parish before he arrives. I recently read one of these letters, a beautiful statement of faith, excitement, and positive impressions of his new parish. He will be warmly welcomed and has already developed political capital that will go a long way as he develops relationships of trust and respect.

2. Are there management tasks to be attended to in the first few weeks and months?

Of course, the new pastor needs to learn about the buildings and property and understand the basic business practices of budgeting, financial protocols, and banking and check signing requirements. Thoroughly understanding the budget is an excellent way to begin to understand the priorities of the parish and how things really work. On the human resources side of management tasks, the first step is to get to know your staff and key volunteers and parish leaders. Does everyone on the staff have a job description? Are there personnel files and do they contain the required basic information about the employee such as compensation, benefits, performance appraisals, and work eligibility forms? If these files do not exist, building those files can be of great assistance in getting to know the staff. Spending time with staff is invaluable.

Attending to these initial management tasks will be greatly facilitated by asking the assistance of the Pastoral Finance Council chair, the school principal, and the parish business manager.

3. Is it true you should not make any substantial changes during the first year?

In many places, new pastors are advised not to make changes for a year. This is both good and bad advice. Changes made too quickly can be disruptive and error-prone because there has not been time for adequate learning and listening. Substantial changes include changes in personnel and Mass schedules, major shifts in budget priorities, or facilities decisions. However, sometimes the previous pastor did not address critical issues, and a new pastor might find that they need immediate attention. The departing pastor may have been ill or aging, and unable to address them. The new pastor must confront them quickly for the well-being of the parish. If change needs to happen more quickly, a wise new pastor will involve others in the decision-making, such as parish pastoral or finance council leadership.

An example I have used in workshops advises against remodeling the rectory in the first few months. But I heard about a situation in which the rectory infrastructure was not sound, the previous pastor smoked and had two cats, and the new pastor had severe allergies. The new pastor brought in the building and grounds committee of the parish finance council to advise him on his next steps. They immediately advised major attention to the rectory, and they announced this as their recommendation. They did not want their new pastor to live in these conditions nor did the parishioners.

Personnel changes are more challenging. The idea that a new pastor needs a new staff is symptomatic of poor management and is an unjust human resources practice. The number-one fear among lay staff at a parish is the arrival of a new pastor. Sometimes a new pastor thinks the staff of the former pastor will not be loyal to him. This dynamic is rare, though at times there are staff members who simply cannot make the adjustment to new leadership and culture. If the new pastor meets with staff members, gets to know them, their skills and their ministerial networks, he may very well learn who will be the most helpful to him in his new assignment and who might not be so helpful. The new pastor has every right to communicate his expectations and direction to the staff, and they have an obligation to align themselves with these expectations and protocols. These changes and adjustments may take time. Jumping to conclusions is rarely helpful.

However, sometimes there are personnel problems that need to be addressed more quickly. For example, people on the staff want to continue working in a style that does not work for the new pastor, such as not keeping to a regular schedule or being present in the office. There may be a crisis with an employee who is causing difficulties on the staff and in the parish that cannot wait for a long adjustment period. Perhaps a secretary/receptionist who speaks a second language is needed quickly because this parish need was not attended to by the previous pastor. There will be some people on a parish staff who will decide in the first few months that the change in pastor created too many incongruities for him or her to continue as part of the parish staff. These changes usually happen naturally, but after enough time has been given for the staff member to make the adjustments, that person may have to be dismissed.

4. Are there special considerations for the new pastor who also has a school to manage?

Parishes with schools are more complex financially and with regards to human resources. The new pastor needs to understand this reality when he accepts his new assignment. The gifts the school brings to the parish are indisputable but there can be problems as well. The new pastor can begin his successful tenure by building a strong, trusting, and respectful relationship with the school principal, who is the professional educator and is committed to the intellectual, emotional, and spiritual development of the children and the staff. The pastor's presence in the school cannot be underestimated. The children need to see him in the school, become used to his presence, and learn especially about liturgy, prayer and the church from him. Faculty and staff will be happy to have him in the school and look to him to help them forge the faith identity of the school. Parents want and need all the help, support, and encouragement they can get from the school staff, the parish, and the pastor. One of his important roles is to encourage all the families to be present for Sunday Mass, practice their faith, and evangelize their children.

THE PASTOR'S PRESENCE IN THE SCHOOL CANNOT BE UNDERESTIMATED.

5. What kind of help can I get if I am the only priest assigned to the parish?

I have often heard pastors say they are "alone" in their parish, meaning there are no other priests assigned there. I understand the sentiment but would like to make a concrete suggestion: Lay ecclesial ministers can offer the kind of sharing in mission and ministry that the pastor may miss by not having an associate pastor or parochial vicar. My friend and colleague Carol Walters, DMin, the director of lay ecclesial ministry for the Archdiocese of Chicago, provided these summary remarks when I asked her this question:

Who are lay ecclesial ministers and what do they do?

Lay ecclesial minister is a generic term used to describe those laypeople who share with pastors "the care of souls" (*Co-Workers in the Vineyard of the Lord*, 55). It is within the purview of each bishop to designate the roles he recognizes as ecclesial ministries. While dioceses may differ in that designation, four characteristics predominate those ministries:

- *Authorization* of the hierarchy to serve publicly in the local church
- *Leadership* in a particular area of ministry
- *Close mutual collaboration* with the pastoral ministry of bishops, priests, and deacons

- *Preparation and formation* appropriate to the level of responsibilities that are assigned to them (*Co-Workers*, 10)

Most lay ecclesial ministers are either full- or part-time employees of a parish. Many have Masters-level degrees and have participated in diocesan or national certification processes to attest to their competence for ministry. Some parish roles that may be included in this designation are pastoral associate, director of religious education, and director of liturgy. Lay ecclesial ministers provide an invaluable contribution to the mission and ministry of the church. While distinct in their roles, they work side by side with their pastors as pastoral leaders in their parishes.

6. To whom should you turn for support, encouragement, and assistance as you begin your new pastorate?

The new pastor will successfully and effectively make the transition if he does not try to do it alone. There are times when he will feel isolated until he forms new friendships and circles of support in his new assignment, but he needs to be connected to others who are willing to listen, encourage, challenge, and accompany him in this new call from God. Very often, this person will be another pastor or classmate. A knowledgeable layperson can also be very helpful. This person should understand church but need not be a parishioner in either the pastor's new or previous parish. Some dioceses have developed pastor mentoring programs, which are very worthwhile if participated in fully. Spiritual direction is also an important practice to continue faithfully during the transition.

The gift of Fr. Dave as the pastor to the parish and parishioners is immense. I have been in church ministry and administration most of my adult life. Without the active support of my respective parishes and pastors, I would never have succeeded and carried on. Fr. Dave and new pastors ought to trust their observations and instincts and believe that God is leading them in their leadership and pastoring of this people of God.

Bibliography

Armstrong, Sharon A., and Barbara Mitchell. *The Essential HR Handbook: A Quick and Handy Resource for Any Manager or HR Professional*. Pompton Plains, NJ: Career Press, 2008.

Augsburger, David W. *Conflict Mediation across Cultures*. Louisville: Westminster John Knox Press, 1992.

Brooks, Rosa E. "Dignity and Discrimination: Toward a Pluralistic Understanding of Workplace Harassment." *The Georgetown Law Journal* 88 (1999): 14–20.

Brounstein, Marty. *Coaching and Mentoring for Dummies*. Hoboken, NJ: Wiley Publishing, 2000.

Byron, William J. *The Power of Principles: Ethics for the New Corporate Culture*. Maryknoll, NY: Orbis Books, 2006.

Castrilli, Michael J., and Charles E. Zech. *Parish Finance: Best Practices in Church Management*. Mahwah, NJ: Paulist Press, 2016.

Clark, William A., and Daniel Gast, eds. *Collaborative Parish Leadership: Contexts, Models, Theology*. Lanham, MD: Lexington Books, 2017.

Clifton, Donald O., Curt Liesveld, and Albert L. Winseman. *Living Your Strengths: Discover Your God Given Talents and Inspire Your Community*. 3rd ed. New York: Gallup Press, 2008.

Clifton, Donald O., and Paula Nelson. *Soar with Your Strengths: A Simple Yet Revolutionary Philosophy of Business and Management*. New York: Dell Trade Paperback, 1992.

DeBerri, Edward, and James Hug. *Catholic Social Teaching: Our Best Kept Secret*. 4th ed. Maryknoll, NY: Orbis Books, 2003.

Fox, Joseph, and Michael W. Caspino. *Model Lay Employee Handbook for Catholic Institutions*. Irvine, CA: Busch & Caspino, n.d.

Garrido, Ann M. *Redeeming Conflict: 12 Habits for Christian Leaders*. Notre Dame: Ave Maria Press, 2016.

Garrido, Ann M., and Gerard Olinger. *Redeeming Administration: 12 Spiritual Habits for Catholic Leaders in Parishes, Schools, Religious Communities, and Other Institutions*. Notre Dame: Ave Maria Press, 2013.

Gula, Richard M. *The Way of Goodness and Holiness: A Spirituality for Pastoral Ministers*. Collegeville, MN: Liturgical Press, 2011.

Hesselbein, Frances. *My Life in Leadership: The Journey and Lessons Learned along the Way*. San Francisco: Jossey-Bass, 2011.

Holmes, Paul A., ed. *A Pastor's Toolbox: Management Skills for Parish Leadership*. Collegeville, MN: Liturgical Press, 2014.

Jewell, Marti R. *Navigating Pastoral Transitions: A Parish Leader's Guide*. Collegeville, MN: Liturgical Press, 2013.

Joint Committee on Taxation. "Present Law and Background Relating to Worker Classification for Federal Tax Purposes (JCX-26-07)," May 7, 2007. https://www.irs.gov/pub/irs-utl/x-26-07.pdf.

Kerkhoff, Barbara. *Navigating Pastoral Transitions: A Staff Guide*. Collegeville, MN: Liturgical Press, 2013.

Lencioni, Patrick. *The Better Pastor*. Sycamore, IL: Lighthouse Catholic Publishing, 2016.

——. *The Five Dysfunctions of a Team*. San Francisco: Jossey-Bass, 2002.

Lowney, Chris. *Everyone Leads: How to Revitalize the Catholic Church*. Lanham, MD: Rowman Littlefield, 2017.

Mallon, James. *Divine Renovation: Bringing Your Parish from Maintenance to Mission*. Toronto: Novalis, 2014.

Marcheschi, Graziano, ed. *Navigating Pastoral Transitions*. Collegeville, MN: Liturgical Press, 2013.

Markham, Donna J. *Spiritlinking Leadership*. New York: Paulist Press, 1991.

Messmer, Max. *Human Resources Kit for Dummies*. Hoboken, NJ: John Wiley & Sons, 2012.

Mitchell, Barbara, and Cornelia Gamlem. *The Big Book of HR*. Revised and updated ed. Wayne, NJ: Career Press, 2017.

Mruk, Edwin S., and William J. Yacullo. "Position Analysis: Executive Search for Catholic Organizations and the Key Ingredient for Success." Whitepaper of Trinity Executive Partnership, Geneva, IL, n.d. http://www.trinityexecutivepartnership.com/white_papers.php.

National Association of Church Personnel Administrators. *The Individual and the Institution*. Cincinnati: NACPA, 1994. http://www.nacpa.org.

——. *Just Treatment for Those Who Work for the Church*. Cincinnati: NACPA, 1986. http://www.nacpa.org.

Paddock, Susan. *Appreciative Inquiry in the Catholic Church*. Plano, TX: Thin Book Publishing, 2003.

Palmer, Parker. *Let Your Life Speak: Listening to the Voice of Vocation*. San Francisco: Jossey-Bass, 1999.

Rath, Tom. *StrengthsFinder 2.0*. New York: Gallup Press, 2007.

Rath, Tom, and Barry Conchie. *Strengths Based Leadership: Great Leaders, Teams, and Why People Follow*. New York: Gallup Press, 2009.

Rojas, Ronald, and John Alvarez. *The Challenges of Pastoral Leadership*. Bloomington, IN: Autor House, 2012.

Romano, Denise. *The HR Toolkit*. New York: McGraw Hill Education, 2010.

Santi, Mary. “Canon Law and Human Resources Policy Development.” Keynote address to National Association of Church Personnel Administrators (NACPA) convocation, April 21, 2015.

Scott, Vivian, and The Dispute Resolution Center of Snohomish and Island Counties. *Conflict Resolution at Work for Dummies*. Hoboken, NJ: John Wiley and Sons, 2010.

Senior, Donald. *The Gift of Administration: New Testament Foundations for the Vocation of Administrative Service*. Collegeville, MN: Liturgical Press, 2015.

Smith, Shawn, and Rebecca Mazin. *The HR Answer Book*. 2nd ed. New York: AMACOM, 2011.

Sofield, Loughlan, and Carol Juliano. *Principled Ministry: A Guidebook for Catholic Church Leaders*. Notre Dame: Ave Maria Press, 2011.

U.S. Equal Employment Opportunity Commission. “Facts about Sexual Harassment.” EEOC. Last modified December 14, 2009. https://www.eeoc.gov/eeoc/publications/fs-sex.cfm.

Weddell, Sherry A. *Forming Intentional Disciples: The Path to Knowing and Following Jesus*. Huntington, IN: Our Sunday Visitor, 2012.

White, Michael, and Tom Corcoran. *Rebuilt: Awakening the Faithful, Reaching the Lost, and Making Church Matter*. Notre Dame: Ave Maria Press, 2013.

Winseman, Albert L. *Growing an Engaged Church: How to Stop “Doing Church” and Start Being the Church Again*. New York: Gallup Press, 2007.

Church Documents

United States Conference of Catholic Bishops. *Co-Workers in the Vineyard of the Lord: A Resource Guide for the Development of Lay Ecclesial Ministry*. Washington, DC: USCCB, 2006.

Evangelii Gaudium (Joy of the Gospel). Apostolic Exhortation of Pope Francis on the Proclamation of the Gospel in Today’s World. Libreria Editrice Vaticana, November 24, 2013.

Laborem Exercens. Encyclical of Pope John Paul II. Libreria Editrice Vaticana, September 14, 1981.

Rerum Novarum (On the Rights and Duties of Capital and Labor). Encyclical of Pope Leo XIII. Libreria Editrice Vaticana, May 15, 1891.

Other Resources and Acknowledgments

Archdiocese of Chicago: Fred Van Den Hende, Director of Human Resources, and Maureen Murphy, Office of Legal Services. Department of Personnel Services Personnel Policies: http://www.archchicago.org.

For more information about a wide range of equal employment opportunity issues, access the EEOC home page at https://www.eeoc.gov/.

Glossary

Age Discrimination: "Age discrimination involves treating an applicant or employee less favorably because of his or her age" (U.S. Equal Employment Opportunity Commission).

Age Discrimination in Employment Act (ADEA): "The Age Discrimination in Employment Act (ADEA) forbids age discrimination against people who are age forty or older. It does not protect workers under the age of forty, although some states have laws that protect younger workers from age discrimination....

The law prohibits discrimination in any aspect of employment, including hiring, firing, pay, job assignments, promotions, layoff, training, benefits, and any other term or condition of employment" (U.S. Equal Employment Opportunity Commission).

Americans with Disabilities Act (ADA): "The Americans with Disabilities Act of 1990 is a civil rights law that prohibits discrimination based on disability. It affords similar protections against discrimination to Americans with disabilities as the Civil Rights Act of 1964, which made discrimination based on race, religion, sex, national origin, and other characteristics illegal. In addition, unlike the Civil Rights Act, the ADA also requires covered employers to provide reasonable accommodations to employees with disabilities, and imposes accessibility requirements on public accommodations" (Wikipedia.org).

Compensatory Time: Comp time, short for compensatory time, is when employers compensate their employees for overtime hours with time off, instead of overtime pay. It is usually illegal for private-sector businesses (including private-sector nonprofit agencies) to compensate overtime-eligible (nonexempt) employees with comp time instead of overtime. These rules are housed under the Fair Labor Standards Act (FLSA).

Comp Time for Exempt Employees: Employers may offer compensatory time for exempt employees, but they are not legally required to do so. Sometimes managers or supervisors grant comp time to exempt employees for rare and major excess hours or days worked.

Corporation Sole: A corporation sole is a legal entity consisting of a single ("sole") incorporated office, occupied by a single ("sole") natural person. This allows corporations such as religious organizations to pass from one office holder to the next, giving the positions legal continuity with subsequent office holders having identical powers and possessions to their predecessors.

Corporation sole originated as a means for orderly transfer of ecclesiastical property. To keep the religious property from being considered the estate of an individual pastor or owned by a congregation, the property title is held by the corporation sole. In the Roman Catholic Church, the title is usually held by the diocesan bishop, who serves in the office of the corporation sole.

Cost of Living Adjustment (COLA): Raises are given to employees for a variety of reasons, such as increased responsibilities or to recognize excellent job performance. Raises are sometimes also awarded to balance inflation, food, health insurance, or transportation costs. These raises are not a result of job performance or value, but rather as a means of treating employees with fairness as cost of living expenses increase. The amounts of such increases are calculated regionally, and the information is widely available to employers. In 2018, the Social Security Administration determined the COLA increase for Social Security recipients would be 2.8 percent.

Employee, Exempt: The Fair Labor Standards Act of 1938 requires that all employees be paid a minimum wage as determined by the federal government and modified by states and municipalities, and compensated for overtime hours worked. Employees not subject to these provisions are *exempt* from these provisions. These exemptions are determined by the job description, for example, those with bona fide executive, administrative, professional, and outside sales responsibilities. There is a duties checklist on the FLSA website or in written details of the law.

Employee, Nonexempt: All employees who do not meet the duties and salary minimum tests in the Fair Labor Standards Act are considered nonexempt and are subject to laws requiring overtime pay and minimum hourly wage.

Employer, At-Will: *At-will employment* is a term used in U.S. labor law for contractual relationships in which an employee can be dismissed by an employer for any reason (i.e., without having to establish "just cause" for termination), and without warning, as long as the reason is not illegal (e.g., firing because of the employee's race or religion). When an employee is acknowledged as being hired "at will," courts deny the employee any claim for loss resulting from the dismissal.

Employer, Just-Cause: In the history of employment practices, just cause standards for termination have become the norm for most employers because there are notable and numerous exceptions to the at-will employment relationship. These exceptions include the number of employees who fall into protected classes of employee status. In faith-based settings, most of the staff are in a protected class of employees vis-à-vis civil rights legislation and other federal protections. Second, there are public policy exceptions such as a prohibition against termination for whistleblowers. Third, contractual employees are not at-will employees, and the courts have increasingly granted an implied contract extension exception for those employees under contract who have had their contracts renewed several times. Likewise, there are long-term employees who may be regarded as implied contractual employees by virtue of their tenure with the employer. Just-cause employers adhere to the standard that involuntary termination will be for a "just cause," not limited to performance, rather than maintain an at-will employment philosophy.

Equal Employment Opportunity Commission (EEOC): Federal legislation that protects the rights of employees is enforced by the EEOC. If an employee judges that he or she has been discriminated against in violation of one of the provisions of federal law that protects employees, a discrimination charge may be filed with the EEOC, who will adjudicate such a claim. The employer has the right to due process and is given the opportunity to respond to such a charge. The EEOC may determine that the charge is valid or may dismiss it. In either case, the employee is given the opportunity to file suit following the decision of the EEOC. The EEOC may also initiate a charge against an employer if information is received that there is a pattern of discrimination or violation of employee rights (Mitchell and Gamlem, *The Big Book of HR*).

Exit Interview: As an employee leaves a position in an organization, especially when the termination is voluntary, it is a best practice to conduct an interview in order to learn the insights and understandings of that employee relative to their tenure with the employer. This interview may be conducted by the person's supervisor, but more often is conducted by a staff member of the Human Resources department. The data from such interviews is collated and analyzed for trends and patterns that may assist the success of the organization and contribute to better retention of staff in the future.

Fair Labor Standards Act of 1938 (FLSA): FLSA is a key piece of federal legislation on compensation norms for all employees of most organizations. There has been significant modifications and development of rules in the implementation of FLSA continuing to the present.

Family and Medical Leave Act of 1993 (FMLA): This is federal legislation requiring an employee be granted an unpaid leave of up to twelve weeks for the birth or adoption of a child, care for a family member with a serious health issue, or the employee's serious health issue. The rights of employees to access FMLA leave provisions is dependent on the size of the employer and the length of time the employee has been with the employer.

Federal Insurance Compensation Act (FICA): FICA is better known as Social Security legislation. This is a mandatory benefit for all except vowed religious. There is some variation in administration for clergy who are regarded as self-employed under the provisions of the law. FICA provides a measure of financial security for employees at retirement or in case of a disability that prevents an individual from employment. This benefit is financed by both employee contributions and employer taxes with a salary cap for taxation that changes each year.

Health Insurance Portability and Accountability Act (HIPPA): HIPPA may be best known for its requirements for privacy in discussing and conveying healthcare information for employees and patients. HIPPA requires great diligence in maintaining confidentiality around all healthcare issues for employees.

HIPPA also makes provision for very limited exclusions for preexisting conditions and prohibits employers and health plans from excluding employees because of their health status (Mitchell and Gamlem, *The Big Book of HR*).

Immigration Reform and Control Act (IRCA): This act requires employers to verify each employee's immigration status and their right to legal employment. Knowingly hiring undocumented workers is illegal.

One of the results is the requirement that employers complete a form for each employee that attests to the inspection of legal documents that ensure the legality of employing an individual. This is known as the I-9 form and must be completed for every new employee. The federal government may inspect employer's files and payroll reports for compliance.

Improvement Plan: Improvement plans for employees are most often developed as the result of a performance appraisal or disciplinary process in which an employee is failing to meet expectations generally or for specific responsibilities. These are written plans with descriptions of the problem(s), suggestions for a process of improvement, criteria for successfully correcting the problems outlined in the plan, and a timeline for feedback and completion.

Independent Contractor: An independent contractor is a person who works in an organization but is not an employee. The independent contractor is responsible for all payroll tax liabilities, including Social Security and Medicare. Whether a person providing a service meets the IRS tests for legitimate independent contractor status is complex and often incorrectly implemented. Further information is available on the website of the U.S. Department of Labor and the Internal Revenue Service, Fact Sheet 13.

Layoff: Layoffs traditionally are rooted in our history of labor relations and unions. However, layoff terminology is commonly used today to indicate involuntary terminations that are usually a reduction in force for financial or organizational reasons. In the union environment. A layoff implies there could be a reinstatement of employment when the reasons for the layoff are resolved. In today's parlance, reinstatement does not ordinally occur and most employees do not expect to return to the workforce with this employer.

Legally Mandated Benefits: Most benefits are not mandatory, that is, the employer is not required to offer them. However, without at least some benefits, it would be very difficult to attract quality staff. Certain benefits are required by federal and state legislation. These include Social Security, Medicare, unemployment insurance, and workers' compensation. Faith-based organizations can be exempt from providing unemployment insurance, but many choose to participate in state plans as a protection for workers.

Medicare: Medicare is a mandatory benefit that provides medical insurance for people age sixty-five and older and for others with certain medical conditions. Clergy and vowed religious can access Medicare under separate provisions.

There are four parts or types of plans for Medicare:

Part A: In-patient hospital care.

Part B: Partial coverage for doctors and other medical services, usually augmented by Medicare clients with privately purchased supplemental insurance.

Part C: Part C is sometimes known as Medicare Advantage. The services of Part A, B, and some other benefits are provided by a provider organization or insurance company. Usually, there is a network of providers that must be used for medical services.

Part D: Prescription drug coverage often supplemented by the individual Medicare client similar to Part B supplements.

Nepotism: Nepotism is the practice of hiring or giving favorable employment treatment to members of one's family. Most organizations have policies that clarify the relationship of employees, regulating their ability to be in a reporting, supervisory, or hiring capacity with members of their families. Such policies also define who is considered "family."

Onboarding: *Onboarding* is another term for new employee orientation. The first few days and weeks are critical learning periods for new employees. Onboarding is the formal process of assimilating a new employee into the organization as a well-functioning member of the staff. New senior leaders in an organization need a longer period of orientation for such assimilation to be successful.

Overtime: Federal and state legislation requires overtime pay for all nonexempt employees who work longer than forty hours in a week. The normal overtime rate is one-and-a-half times one's regular hourly rate for time worked over forty hours. Overtime calculations can be complex and payroll professionals are usually involved in the administration of overtime.

Performance Appraisals: The formal tools used in a performance management system are called performance appraisals. There are many types of appraisals available to employers, and these tools are used periodically at the discretion of the employer. Normally, appraisal tools are used at least annually, and often more frequently.

Performance Management: Performance management includes all the methods and practices used in an organization to assure the best possible outcomes and implementation of mission. Performance appraisal tools are one of the means used to monitor employee performance. Onboarding, supervision, training, planning, job descriptions, clear success criteria, and feedback systems are all part of performance management. Performance management is a critical piece of management if the organization believes in its mission and works toward the most effective possible implementation of that mission.

Progressive Discipline: Processes for correcting problem behaviors or attitudes are often outlined in employee handbooks. While there are circumstances in which progressive discipline is not appropriate, these processes are used when the employer's goal is to inform the employee of a problem and suggest clear means for correcting the behavior. Steps in progressive discipline may include conversation with the employee (recorded in a memo to the employee and placed in his or her file), written warnings, suspension with or without pay, and ending with resignation or involuntary termination.

Reduction in Force: When an organization must decrease the number of its employees for financial or mission-related reasons, a reduction in force is the process. This is sometimes referred to as a layoff.

Reorganization: From a human resources perspective, a reorganization of staff sometimes results in terminations of one or several employees. The reorganization is a realignment of positions, new job descriptions, and the possible elimination of one or more positions. Sometimes what is called reorganization is, in fact, one or more involuntary terminations done under the guise of reorganization but without meeting clear standards of reorganization.

Salary Structure: Many employers establish a salary structure with stated ranges and most of the positions in the organization named in one of those ranges. Salary structures are constructed by careful analyses of job descriptions and required skills for implementation of those job descriptions. A compensation system is developed from this. These are often developed with the help of outside experts and consultants.

Succession Planning: Succession planning is anticipating the normal changes in workforces to ensure transitions in staff without significant interruption to the mission, goals, and strategic plan implementation of the organization.

Termination, Involuntary: Involuntary termination is ending the employment of one or more employees of an organization against their will. Involuntary terminations include reductions in force, at-will termination, and termination for cause.

Termination, Voluntary: Voluntary termination is ending the employment relationship as a result of an employee's decision to leave the organization. Voluntary terminations include resignation and retirement.

Termination for Cause: Ending an employment relationship for cause includes cases of poor performance, violation of policy, violations of the law, or behaviors and attitudes that undermine the mission of the organization or its moral, ethical, legal, and policy standards.

Title VI of the Civil Rights Act of 1964: Title VI prohibits employers from discriminating based on race, color, religion, gender, or national origin in any employment practice, including hiring, termination, discipline, compensation, training, promotion, benefits, and terms and conditions and privileges of employment. Church employers are exempt from the provisions of disclination based on religion.

Total Rewards: A term used by many employers, *total rewards* refer to all the ways by which an employee is rewarded or compensated for his or her work for the organization. Total rewards statements include salary, bonuses, benefits, paid time off, professional development, and employer taxes paid by the organization on behalf of each employee, such as Medicare and FICA. There are also less tangible means of compensation such as organizational culture, consistent respect of the employee, assistance with career development, and, for church organizations, the opportunity for spiritual development.

Unemployment Insurance: Unemployment insurance is a mandated benefit for most organizations but is not mandated for church employers. This is a state administered program that provides a safety net for employees who are involuntarily terminated. It is a percentage of wages or salary for a limited period and is normally financed by taxation of employers based on their prior unemployment experience. Church employers who choose to participate often do so on a reimbursable system in which the state bills the church employer for the cost of the unemployment paid to the terminated employee.

W-4: This is an IRS form that every employee completes at the beginning of his or her employment, which determines the amount of money the employer will withhold from each pay check and remit to the IRS on behalf of the employee. The employee can change the information on his or her W-4 when financial or family circumstances change. All employees must withhold estimated taxes every pay period as well as for bonuses paid. Clergy are not required to withhold taxes. They may pay quarterly estimated taxes instead of withholding each pay period.

Workers' Compensation: Workers' compensation is a mandated benefit normally administered through the employer's property and liability insurance. This insurance provides assistance to an employee who has been injured or falls ill as a result of a workplace incident or condition. Medical expenses are covered as well as compensation replacement.

Index